THE CORGI CALORIE COUNTER

THE CORGI
CALORIE
COUNTER

ANNE BEWLEY

CORGI BOOKS

THE CORGI CALORIE COUNTER
A CORGI BOOK 0 552 13186 5

First publication in Great Britain

PRINTING HISTORY
Corgi edition published 1989
Corgi edition reprinted 1989
Corgi edition reprinted 1991

This book is set in Linotype Gill by Goodfellow & Egan Ltd., Cambridge

Corgi Books are published by Transworld Publishers Ltd., 61–63 Uxbridge Road, Ealing, London W5 5SA, in Australia by Transworld Publishers (Australia) Pty. Ltd., 15–23 Helles Avenue, Moorebank, NSW 2170, and in New Zealand by Transworld Publishers (N.Z.) Ltd., Cnr. Moselle and Waipareira Avenues, Henderson, Auckland.

Printed and bound in Great Britain by
Cox & Wyman Ltd., Reading, Berks.

CONTENTS

DRINK

ACKNOWLEDGEMENTS

Many of the calorific values in this book are taken from *The Composition of Foods* by R. A. McCance and E. M. Widdowson, fourth revised and extended edition of the Medical Research Council Special Report No 297 by A. A. Paul and D. A. T. Southgate published by HMSO, Crown copyright 1978, third impression 1985.

The author would also like to thank Susan Collins for all her help with the project, together with Clare Whittaker.

INTRODUCTION

One of the most popular ways to control weight is to limit the number of calories that you take in each day. Counting is not difficult and the results from a calorie-controlled diet are often more satisfactory than those achieved on one of the crash diets. Despite the ever-growing number of meal replacement foods that come on to the market, many people return to the simple method of counting the calories each day in the foods that they eat to achieve success in weight control. This book is for them.

A calorie is simply a unit of energy. The body requires a certain number each day to function. Using up the same number of units a day as you consume in food means that your weight should remain constant. To lose weight, the balance has to be tipped. Each of us has a different metabolic rate. Someone doing a job which requires a considerable amount of physical labour will burn up more units of energy than someone who sits at an office desk all day. For a woman the average number of calories used up in a day varies from 2,250 to 1,750. For a man, the number varies from 3,500 to 2,500. When first going on to a calorie-controlled diet it is sensible to aim at eating foods that contain 250 calories less than the average for a couple of weeks; if you lose 1–2 kg

(2–3½ lb) in the first week and slightly less in the second week, that should be satisfactory. It is probable that you will lose extra fluid from the body during the first week, which explains why the weight loss is greater. By eating 250 calories fewer than you use up, it is probable that you will break down approximately 25 g (1 oz) of solid fat from the body's stores.

If at the end of two weeks you have not lost weight, then the number of calories you take in each day should be cut slightly more, say by 400 units a day.

Tips for weight loss

*Try to eat your main meal in the middle of the day. This gives you the rest of the day in which to expend energy and use up the calories you have consumed. Fewer calories are used up when you are asleep.

*Eat food slowly. This has the effect of making you feel more satisfied than if you gobble food in a rush.

*Keep a weekly chart of your progress. This is encouraging and should help to stop you breaking your diet. Do not rush to the scales every day as this can be disappointing.

*Keep to a healthy diet, a well-balanced mixture of protein, carbohydrate and fats. It is wise to cut down on carbohydrates and fatty foods as these tend to contain more calories but do not exclude them altogether, as they are essential in some measure to good health.

*Never nibble in between meals, and try to make yourself as

varied a diet as possible; this can help you to avoid temptation.

*Do not worry if you exceed your allowance of calories one day; you can compensate for it the next day by reducing your intake by the total over-consumed. But do not allow this to happen frequently. Be honest with yourself.

*Weight loss occurs when you eat less. In other words, to lose weight you need to reduce your intake of calories.

I hope that you find this book helps you.

NOTE

The products in this book have been arranged into groups such as Biscuits, Bread, Burgers, Confectionery, Diabetic, Meat, Simply for Slimmers, Soups, Vegetarian in the Food Section and Beer & Lager, Crushes, Hot Drinks, Slimmers' and Health Drinks, Wines in the Drink Section.

Where a product is made by several manufacturers I have included a range of them, particularly those where the calorific content varies from one manufacturer to another. I should like to thank all the manufacturers who have kindly helped by providing calorie counts for this book.

WHAT YOU SHOULD WEIGH

This is a mean average of what you should weigh and may be helpful in giving you a target to work to. Large or small-framed people can add or deduct weight from these figures, but be sure you do not cheat.

WOMEN

4ft 10in	1.47m	7st 3lb	45.5 kg
4ft 11in	1.50m	7st 6lb	47.0 kg
5ft	1.52m	7st 9lb	48.5 kg
5ft 1in	1.55m	7st 12lb	50.0 kg
5ft 2in	1.57m	8st 1lb	51.0 kg
5ft 3in	1.60m	8st 4lb	52.5 kg
5ft 4in	1.63m	8st 7lb	54.0 kg
5ft 5in	1.65m	8st 11lb	55.75kg
5ft 6in	1.68m	9st 1lb	57.5 kg
5ft 7in	1.70m	9st 5lb	59.25kg
5ft 8in	1.73m	9st 9lb	61.0 kg
5ft 9in	1.75m	9st 13lb	63.0 kg
5ft 10in	1.78m	10st 3lb	64.5 kg
5ft 11in	1.80m	10st 7lb	66.5 kg
6ft	1.83m	10st 11lb	68.5 kg

MEN

5ft 2in	1.57m	8st 11lb	55.5kg
5ft 3in	1.60m	9st 1lb	57.5kg
5ft 4in	1.63m	9st 4lb	59.0kg
5ft 5in	1.65m	9st 7lb	60.0kg
5ft 6in	1.68m	9st 10lb	61.5kg
5ft 7in	1.70m	10st	63.5kg
5ft 8in	1.73m	10st 5lb	65.5kg
5ft 9in	1.75m	10st 9lb	67.5kg
5ft 10in	1.78m	10st 13lb	69.5kg
5ft 11in	1.80m	11st 3lb	71.0kg
6ft	1.83m	11st 8lb	73.5kg
6ft 1in	1.85m	11st 12lb	75.0kg
6ft 2in	1.88m	12st 3lb	77.5kg
6ft 3in	1.90m	12st 8lb	79.5kg
6ft 4in	1.93m	12st 13lb	82.0kg

FOOD

	g	oz	Cal.

BISCUITS, SAVOURY AND CRISPBREADS

Bran Crispbread, GG Scandinavian Suppliers	each			12
Bran or Sesame Thin Crispbread, Ideal	each			15
Brown Crispbread, Ryvita	each			25
Brown Rye/Fibre plus Crispbread, Ry-King	each			30
Butter Puff, Crawfords	each			45
Carr's Table Water Biscuit: large	each			30
small	each			16
Cheddar Savoury Biscuit, Crawfords	each			22
Cheese & Celery Sticks Biscuit, Huntley & Palmer	each			22
Cheeselets, Peak Frean	each			3
Cheese Sandwich Biscuit, Waitrose	each			45
Cheese Savor Biscuit, Crawfords	each			3
Cheese Thins, Gateway		28	1	152

	g	oz	Cal.
Cracker Barrel Biscuit, Kraft	28	1	120
Cream Cracker Biscuit:			
Crawfords each			33
Waitrose each			30
Energen slice			18
Extra Thin Crispbread, Primula slice			17
High Baked Water Biscuit, Tesco each			25
Krackawheat Biscuit, McVitie's each			38
Light Crispbread:			
Ry-King each			25
Nisa each			15
Macvita Crispbread, McVitie's each			35
Ritz Savoury Biscuit, Sainsbury each			16
Savours Savoury Biscuit, Crawford packet	35	1¼	195
Scanda Crips, GG Scandinavian Suppliers slice			18
Sesame Cracker, Waitrose each			20
Table Water Biscuit, Carr's:			
large each			30
small each			16
Tuc, Savoury Sandwich Biscuit, McVitie's each			73

	g	oz	Cal.
Water High Bake Biscuit, Jacobs	each		26
Wheat Crackers, Tesco	each		40
Whole Grain Crispbread, Ideal	each		10
Wholemeal Bran Biscuit, St Michael	each		67
Wholemeal Cracker, Fox's	each		40
Wholemeal Crispbread, Country Basket	each		28

BISCUITS, SWEET

	g	oz	Cal.
Abbey Crunch, McVitie's	each		47
Abernethy, McVitie's	each		45
All Butter Shortbread Finger, St Michael	each		110
All Butter Crunch, Sainsbury	each		30
Almond Flavour Snapjack Cream, Burtons	each		70
Almond, Waitrose	each		50
Almond & Honey, McVitie's	each		86
Balmoral Finger, Crawfords	each		68
Bandit, McVitie's	each		103

	g	oz	Cal.
Bargain Bag Choc Chip & Hazelnut Cookies, Crawfords	each			40
Big Bar Bandit, McVitie's	each			215
Big 5 Caramel Wafer, Spar	28	1	136
Bourbon Cream, Peak Frean	each			56
Bournville Digestive, Cadbury	each			45
Bournville Sandwich, Cadbury	each			120
Braemar, Huntley & Palmer	each			49
Bran, Boots	each			45
Bran Crunch, Fox's	each			30
Brandy Snap, St Michael	each			25
Breakaway, Rowntree Mackintosh	each			105
Butter Crinkle, Safeway	each			36
Butter Crunch, St Michael	each			65
Butterscotch Teamates, Paterson	each			60
Butter Shortie, Fox's	each			30
Caramel Cookie Ring, Tesco	each			46
Caramel Wafer, Tunnocks	each			125
Caramel Wafer, Mackintosh	each			85
Carob Chip, Prewetts	each			85

	g	oz	Cal.
Catherine Wheels, Fry's	28	1	88
Choc 'n' Nut Cookie, Gateway	each		52
Chocolate Biscuit Finger, milk or plain, McVitie's	each		25
Chocolate Chip Cookie, Waitrose	each		15
Chocolate Digestive, plain, McVitie's	each		98
Chocolate Homewheat, milk or plain, McVitie's	each		84
Chocolate Shortcake, Gateway	each		95
Club, plain, Jacob's	each		110
Club, wafer, Jacob's	each		104
Coconut Crumble Cream, Waitrose	each		72
Coconut Macaroon, Tesco	each		55
Coconut Mallow, Peak Frean	each		46
Coconut Rings, Tesco	each		46
Coffee Cream, Peak Frean	each		57
Cookie Coaster, Cadbury	each		52
Country Crunch, Peak Frean	each		30
Crunch Cream, Peak Frean	each		57

	g	oz	Cal.
Currant Crisp, Peak Frean	each		30
Custard Cream, Tesco	each		60
Devon Cream, Peak Frean	each		55
Digestive:			
Bejam	each		65
Burtons	each		50
Bournville, Cadbury	each		45
Chocolate, Huntley & Palmer	each		60
Chocolate, Sainsbury	each		55
Fruit, Huntley & Palmer	each		50
Hovis	each		55
Huntley & Palmer	each		65
McVitie's	each		75
Milk chocolate: Cadbury	each		50
St Michael	each		65
Sainsbury	each		65
Plain chocolate: St Michael	each		65
Dutch Finger, St Michael	each		50
Garibaldi, Peak Frean	each		30
Ginger Cream, Fox's	each		65
Ginger Nut, McVitie's	each		45
Ginger Snap, Sainsbury	each		40
Girdle Oatcakes, Paterson	each		55
Golden Crunch Cream, Safeway	each		70
Granny Ann High Fi, Itona	each		90

BISCUITS

	g	oz	Cal.
Gypsy Cream, McVitie's each			68
Hazelnut, Boots each			30
Hazelnut & Raisin Country Cookies, McVitie's each			82
Healthy Life, Mitchell Hill each			61
Highland Finger, McVitie's each			65
Honey, Allinson each			55
Iced Gem, Peak Frean each			3
Iced Shorties, Crawford's Balmoral each			40
Jaffa Cake: McVitie's each			45
Sainsbury each			50
Jaffa Crunch, Peak Frean each			30
Jamboree Mallow, Peak Frean each			75
Jam Sandwich Cream, Fox's each			70
Jersey Cream, Peak Frean each			55
Lemon Crisp, Burtons each			30
Lemon Crumble Cream, Spar	28	1	147
Lemon Marshmallows, Barker & Dobson	28	1	92
Lemon Puff, Sainsbury each			75
Lincoln, McVitie's each			46

FOOD

	g	oz	Cal.
Malted Milk Chocolate Bar, Elkes	each		95
Malted Crunch Cream, Fox's	each		58
Marie, Crawfords	each		29
Milk Chocolate Finger, Safeway	each		46
Milk Chocolate Orange Finger, Safeway	each		40
Milk Chocolate Assorted, Cadbury	each		62
Milk Chocolate Petite Beurre, Sainsbury	each		50
Milk Chocolate Tea Cake, St Michael	each		80
Muesli, Allinson	each		62
Muesli Fruit, Boots	each		40
Muesli Slice, Holly Mills	each		216
Munchmallow, McVitie's	each		81
Neapolitan Wafer, Peak Frean	each		37
Nice Cream, Peak Frean	each		45
Oatcakes, average	28	1	125
Oaten Crunch, Fox's	each		35
Oatflake & Honey Cookie, Burtons	each		50

	g	oz	Cal.
Oat & Fruit, Fox's	each		75
Oatmeal: Allinson	each		60
Country Basket	each		35
Oatmeal Crunch, Sainsbury	each		30
Orange Cream:			
Cadbury	each		80
Crawfords	each		58
Peak Frean	each		55
Orange Milk Chocolate Waifa, Terry's	each		180
Orange Viscount, Burton's	each		90
Original Thick Tea, Fox's	each		60
Penguin, McVitie's	each		130
Petticoat Tail, McVitie's	each		57
Picnic Bar, Cadbury	each		220
Plain Chocolate Wafer, Terry's	each		175
Plain Ginger, St Michael	each		45
Rich Highland Shortie, Nisa	each		50
Rich Shortie, Bejam	each		50
Rich Tea: Burton's	each		36
Sainsbury	each		45
Rich Tea Finger Cream, St Michael	each		50

		g	oz	Cal.
Sesame and Sunflower, Prewetts	each			85
Shortbread Fingers, Littlewoods	each			95
Shortbread Round, Paterson	each			500
Shortie, Safeway	each			50
Shortcake: Bejam	each			50
Presto	each			60
Six Grain, Boots Second Nature, Wholemeal	each			40
Snapjack, Burtons	each			72
Snowball: Burtons	each			90
Sainsbury	each			105
Solitaire Shortbread, Fox's	each			45
Sponge Finger, Huntley & Palmer	each			20
Sport, Fox's	each			30
Stem Ginger, Prewetts	each			70
Stem Ginger, Crinkle, Fox's	each			80
Sultana and Spice Cream, Waitrose	each			65
Sunnybisk, Granose	each			70
Tartan Shortbread, Crawfords	each			82

	g	oz	Cal.
Tea Finger, Sainsbury	each		25
Thick Finger Shortbread, Burton's	each		103
Thin Arrowroot, Crawfords	each		31
Thistle Shortbread, Burton's	each		105
Traditional Coconut Cookie, Fox's	each		75
Traditional Ginger Cookie, Fox's	each		65
Traditional Oatcake Cookie, Fox's	each		70
Treacle Crunch, Burton's	each		45
Treacle Crunch Cream, Fox's	each		65
Trio, Jacob's	each		132
United Extra Time, McVitie's	each		223
United Orange, McVitie's	each		111
Wafer Snack, Cadbury	each		65
Wafer Delight, Huntley & Palmer	each		97
Walnut, Allinson	each		85
Wheatmeal, McVitie's	each		73
Wholemeal, Simmers Healthy Life Range	each		74

	g	oz	Cal.
Wholemeal Shortbread, Boots Second Nature Biscuits	each		100
Wholewheat, Waitrose	28	1	98
Yoghurt, Country Basket	each		34
Yo Yo, McVitie's: mint	each		98
toffee	each		86

BREAD

	g	oz	Cal.
Big Country Bread, St Michael	28	1	73
Black rye	28	1	94
Bran Breadmix, Allinson	packet		2045
Brown	28	1	63
Currant	28	1	70
Fried in lard	slice 28	1	160
French	slice 28	1	85
Fruit Bread, Granose	28	1	85
Fruit sesame	28	1	120
Granary	slice 28	1	70
HiBran, Vitbe, small loaf	slice		50
High Fibre Wholemeal Loaf	slice		71
Hovis Wheat Slice, Hovis	slice		24

		g	oz	Cal.
Laver		28	1	15
Malted Wheat Cob, Sainsbury		28	1	70
Milk	slice			86
Mix, Allinson	packet			2045
Nut Loaf, Granose		425	15	750
Pumpernickel	slice	28	1	64
Rye, Sainsbury	slice	28	1	28
Rye-Bran, Primula: extra thin	slice			15
thick	slice			19
Rye Extra Thin, Sainsbury	slice	28	1	20
Rye Flour Bread Mix, Prewetts		28	1	84
Soda, white	slice			80
Sunmalt Loaf, Sunblest		28	1	75
Wheatgerm	slice			70
Wheatmeal Bread Mix, Granny Smith	pack			835
White		28	1	69
White Bread Mix, Granny Smith	pack			1000
Wholemeal, average		28	1	78
Wholemeal, 100%	slice			66
Wholemeal Loaf, Boots		28	1	61

		g	oz	Cal.
Wholemeal Bread Mix, Allinson	pack			1865
Long Nimble Bread, Nimble	slice			35
Breadcrumbs: dried	15ml/1 tablespoon			30
fresh	15ml/1 tablespoon			8

BREAD ROLLS AND BUNS

		g	oz	Cal.
Bagel	each	40	1½	150
Bap	each	40	1½	135
Bath bun	each	40	1½	122
Breadstick	each			15
Bridge roll	each	15	½	35
Brioche	each	40	1½	196
Burger Bun, Bejam	each			125
Chelsea bun	each	90	3¼	250
Croissant	each	40	1½	165
Crumpet, toasted	each	40	1½	75
Currant bun	each	40	1½	137
French toast	slice			50
Hot cross bun	each	40	1½	160
Hovis roll	each	40	1½	100
Mild garlic roll, Sainsbury		28	1	76

		g	oz	Cal.
Muffin	each	60	2¼	125
Pitta	standard	70	2½	186
Roll, Energen	each			25
Scone, white	each	50	2	206
Teacake	each	50	2	152
Savoury bun, Daloon	pack			130

BURGERS

		g	oz	Cal.
American Hamburger, Brooks	each			315
Baconburger, Wimpy	each			302
Baked Beans with Hamburgers, Chef		28	1	34
Beefburger:				
average minus bun		28	1	55
Birds Eye, Original	each			120
100%	each			120
Freshbake	each			165
Market Choice, Economy	each			134
Waitrose, frozen		28	1	50
Big Mac with Bun, McDonald's	each			560
Burger, Birds Eye Economy	each			100
Cheeseburger with Bun, McDonald's	each			300

	g	oz	Cal.
Cheeseburger with Bun, Wimpy — each			280
Egg 'n' Baconburger, Wimpy — each			410
Fish Burgers, Birds Eye — each			95
Hamburger:			
Danish Prime — each			120
in gravy, Tesco — tinned	28	1	41
Waitrose — each, frozen			146
with Bun, McDonald's — each			250
Minceburger, cooked without fat:			
Birds Eye — each			100
Quarter Pounder with Bun, McDonald's — each			420
Quarter Pounder with Cheese & Bun, McDonald's — each			525
Rather Special Beefburgers, McLaren — each			204
Turkey & Beefburger, Matthew's, grilled with no fat — each			270
Wimpy Hamburger with bun, Wimpy — each			240
Wimpy Half-pounder in bun, Wimpy — each			880
Wimpy Quarter-pounder with bun, Wimpy — each			530

		g	oz	Cal.
Wimpy Quarter-pounder with bun & cheese, Wimpy	each			575

CAKES AND SCONES

		g	oz	Cal.
All Butter Madeira & Walnut Cake, St Michael		28	1	113
All Butter Walnut Sandwich Cake, Sainsbury, large	each			930
Almond Slice, Sainsbury	each			130
Angel Layer Cake, Mr Kipling, large	each			1125
Apple & Blackcurrant Puff Pastry, Lyons	each			185
Apricot Madeleine, Lyons, small cake	each			115
Apricot Sponge Roll, St Michael		28	1	100
Bakewell Slice, Mr Kipling, small cake	each			175
Bakewell Slice, Green's mix	packet			1505
Battenburg, Lyons, large	each			990
Bisquick, Betty Crocker mix	packet			4800
Blackcurrant Sponge Curl, Mr Kipling, small	each			195

		g	oz	Cal.
Blackcurrant Sponge Roll, Lyons	each			980
Black Forest Gâteau:				
Birds Eye, large	each			1500
Mary Baker Simply Sweet				
mix, Nabisco Frear	each			1470
Brandy Cake, Lyons, large	tinned			2620
Buttercream Walnut Cake, Mr Kipling	each			1330
Butterfly Tops, Mary Baker Simply Sweet mix, Nabisco Frear	pack			840
Butter Madeira Cake:				
St Michael, large	each	28	1	114
Lyons	each			760
Carnival, Viota cake mix	each			66
Cherry Fruit Cake, Cadbury		28	1	87
Cherry or Genoa Fruit Pieces, McVitie's		28	1	98
Cherry Shortcake, Mary Baker mix, Nabisco Frear	packet			1383
Cherry Slice, Mr Kipling	each			140
Chocolate Cake, Cadbury		28	1	112
Chocolate Fudge Cake, Cadbury		28	1	103

	g	oz	Cal.
Chocolate Gâteau Roule, Waitrose	28	1	104
Chocolate Sponge Sandwich Cake, Tesco	each		700
Coconut Macaroon, Mr Kipling small cake	each		106
Coffee Gâteau, Mr Kipling large cake	28	1	106
Corn Crisp, Waitrose	28	1	105
Cup Cake, Lyons: chocolate	each		129
orange & cream	each		129
Currant cake, average	28	1	119
Cut Cherry Genoa Cake, Safeway	28	1	90
Cut Sultana Cake, Safeway	28	1	102
Dark Chocolate Fudge Creamy Fostings Cake, Betty Crocker mix	packet		2040
Date Loaf, Green's mix	packet		1420
Devils Food Cake, Betty Crocker mix	packet		3000
Devon Flavourmoist Cake, Green's mix	packet		1875
Dundee Cake, Sainsbury, large	each		1100

	g	oz	Cal.
Eccles Cake, Sainsbury	each			190
Economix Chocolate Sponge Cake, Viota mix	packet			1075
Flake Cake, Cadbury	each			125
Fondant Fancy Cake: St Michael	each			108
Sainsbury	each			106
French Fancy, Mr Kipling small cakes	each			103
Fruit Loaf: Green's mix	packet			1390
Mary Baker Simply Sweet mix	packet			1190
Fruity Malt Loaf, Sainsbury		28	1	74
Fudge Brownie Mix, Betty Crocker mix	packet			2400
Fudge Brownies, Mr Kipling	each			155
Genoa Cake, Sainsbury, large	each			1190
German Chocolate Cake, Betty Crocker mix	packet			3120
Ginger Cake, Viota mix	packet			975
Gingerbread, average		28	1	105
Gingerbread Men, Sainsbury, small	each			145
Golden Shred Orange Marmalade Cake, Viota mix	packet			1120

	g	oz	Cal.
Hazelnut Cake, Green's mix, made up	packet			1875
Iced All Butter Madeira Cake, St Michael	28	1	110
Iced Bavarian Cake, Green's luxury mix	packet			2125
Iced Fairy Cakes, Viota mix	packet			1040
	each			65
Iced Fruit Cake, Sainsbury, large	each			1190
Iced Madeira Sandwich Cake, Waitrose, large	28	1	117
Iced Rich Fruit Cake, Tesco	each			1260
Iced Walnut Cake, Green's luxury mix	packet			2140
Jaffa Finger, Mr Kipling small cake	each			130
Jamaica Ginger Cake:				
Lyons large	each			1030
Mr Kipling	each			920
Jam Swiss Roll, Mr Kipling	each			505
Junior Choc Roll, Cadbury:				
with caramel filling	each			105
with raspberry filling	each			94
Junior Jam Roll, Sainsbury	each			70

		g	oz	Cal.
Kensington Piece, McVitie's		340	12	1205
Kensington Slab, McVitie's	slice	50	2	206
Lemon Cake Mix, Betty Crocker mix	packet			3120
Lemon Cup Cakes with water icing, Viota mix	packet			995
Lemon Madeira Cake, Granny Smith mix	each			915
Lemon Tops, Nabisco mix	each			830
Luxury Sponge Cake, Granny Smith mix	packet			1000
Madeira Cake: Green's mix	packet			1477
Mr Kipling	each			1042
Manor House Cake, Mr Kipling	each			1600
Marzipan Top Christmas Cake, McVitie's		28	1	78
Meringue Nest, St Michael	each			62
Milk Chocolate Cake, Betty Crocker mix	packet			2030
Milk Chocolate Eclairs, Cadbury		28	1	125
Milk Chocolate Sponge Mallow, St Michael	each			90
Mince Puff Pastry, Lyons	each			184

	g	oz	Cal.
Mini Roll, Cadbury	each		114
Mini Swiss Roll, Sainsbury	each		144
Orange cake, plain, average	28	1	132
Orange Frosted Cake, Viota mix, made up	packet		1060
Orange & Lemon Slice:			
Barker & Dobson	28	1	100
Pearce Duff mix	28	1	80
Waitrose	28	1	30
Orange Tops, Mary Baker mix	packet		831
Parkin Cut Cake, St Michael, large	28	1	93
Plain Sponge Cake, Green's mix	packet		748
Queen's cake, average	28	1	129
Queen Victoria Sponge Cake, Lyons, frozen	each		910
Red Cherry Butter Sponge Cake, Tiffany's	each		300
Regal Swiss Roll, Mr Kipling	each		850
Rice Crisp Cake with Raisins, St Michael	each		90
Rock Cake:			
Green's traditional mix	packet		1130
Viota mix	packet		1270

	g	oz	Cal.
Scone with Fresh Cream, St Michael	each		180
Scone, Granny Smith mix	packet		865
Snowball, St Michael	each		105
Sour Cream Chocolate Fudge Cake, Betty Crocker mix	packet		2040
Spicy Mix Cake, Granny Smith	packet		960
Sponge Gâteau, Sainsbury, large	each		1120
Swiss Gâteau, Cadbury	each		1025
Swiss Roll:			
black cherry & buttercream, Sainsbury, large	each		840
Cadbury	each		865
chocolate angel cake, Sainsbury	28	1	120
chocolate, Lyons	each		630
jam & vanilla, Lyons	each		625
raspberry, Sainsbury	each		390
Teacakes, Viota mix	packet		1320
Trifle Sponge Cake, Lyons	each		80
Triple Decker, Lyons large	each		640
Tunis Cake, McVitie's	28	1	128
Vanilla Sandwich Cake, Mary Baker mix	packet		1370

	g	oz	Cal.
Victoria Sponge Cake, Green's mix	packet		1400
Victoria Sponge Cake, Cadbury	28	1	64
Viennese Cake, St Michael, all butter	each		283
Walnut & Buttercream Cake, Sainsbury	each		1222
Walnut Layer Cake:			
Viota mix, large	packet		1247
Waitrose	28	1	121
Wholemeal Scone Round, Mr Kipling	each		1197
Yellow Cake, Betty Crocker mix	packet		3000

CAKE DECORATIONS AND BAKING INGREDIENTS

		g	oz	Cal.
Angelica		28	1	90
Chocolate vermicelli		28	1	135
Coconut, desiccated		28	1	171
Crunch Base, Granny Smith mix		28	1	135
Baking powder	1 teaspoon			5
		28	1	45

	g	oz	Cal.
Butter Pecan Creamy Frosting, Betty Crocker mix packet			204
Flour:			
brown	28	1	90
buckwheat	28	1	100
cornmeal, 96%	28	1	103
60%	28	1	100
cassava	28	1	97
granary	28	1	99
maizemeal, 96%	28	1	103
60%	28	1	100
rice	28	1	100
rye	28	1	95
soya: full fat	28	1	127
low fat	28	1	100
wheatmeal	28	1	93
white: plain	28	1	99
self-raising	28	1	96
strong	28	1	96
wholemeal	28	1	90
yam	28	1	90
Fondant Icing, Whitworth's, vanilla	28	1	110
Hundreds & thousands, average 1 teaspoon			15
Jelly Crystals, Pearce Duff packet			180
Jelly Diamonds, Pearce Duff	28	1	80
Kake Drops, Kakebrand	28	1	155

	g	oz	Cal.
Marzipan, average	28	1	125
Polka Dots, Lyons Tetley: milk packet			575
plain packet			585
Simply Topping, Royal packet			485
Sugar Flowers, Pearce Duff	28	1	105
Vanilla Top 'n' Fill, Homepride sachet	220	7¾	940
Yeast: dried	28	1	48
fresh	28	1	15

CEREALS

	g	oz	Cal.
All-Bran, Kellogg's	28	1	80
Alpen, Weetabix	28	1	105
Alpen Porridge, Weetabix	28	1	110
Alpen with Tropical Fruit, Weetabix	28	1	109
Apple & Banana Bran Brek, Holly Mills	28	1	125
Barley, pearl, average: boiled	28	1	34
raw 1 tablespoon			45
Bran, average	28	1	58
Bran Buds, Kellogg's	28	1	77
Bran Fare, Weetabix	28	1	65

		g	oz	Cal.
Bran Flakes, Co-op		28	1	98
Bran Muesli, Prewetts		28	1	90
Breakfast Biscuit, Nisa	each			55
Breakfast Oats, Prewetts		28	1	110
Breakfast Bran, Sainsbury		28	1	75
Breakfast Special, St Michael		28	1	98
Buckwheat		28	1	28
Cornflakes, Kellogg's		28	1	99
Coco Pops, Kellogg's		28	1	101
Crunchy Bran, Allinson		28	1	63
Crunchy Nut Cornflakes, Kellogg's		28	1	107
Cubs		28	1	101
Deluxe Muesli, Sunwheel Foods		28	1	110
Force Wheat Flakes		28	1	105
Flour:				
brown		28	1	90
buckwheat		28	1	100
cornmeal, 96%		28	1	103
60%		28	1	100
cassava		28	1	97
granary		28	1	99
maizemeal, 96%		28	1	103
60%		28	1	100

	g	oz	Cal.
rice	28	1	100
rye	28	1	95
soya: full fat	28	1	127
low fat	28	1	100
wheatmeal	28	1	93
white: plain	28	1	99
self-raising	28	1	96
strong	28	1	96
wholemeal	28	1	90
yam	28	1	90
Frosties, Kellogg's	28	1	101
Golden Crunch Breakfast, Mapleton's	28	1	24
Golden Grains Breakfast, Prewetts	28	1	105
Grape Nuts, Bird's	28	1	100
Harvest Break, Nabisco Frear	portion		220
Harvest Crunch, Bran & Apple, Quaker	28	1	29
Honey Smacks, Kellogg's	28	1	99
Hot Bran, Quaker	28	1	92
Hot Oat with Bran, Sainsbury	28	1	95
Instant Hot Oat Cereal, Sainsbury	28	1	110
Instant Porridge, Waitrose	28	1	115

	g	oz	Cal.
Maize	28	1	103
Muesli: average	28	1	106
Boots	28	1	105
Oat Krunchies	28	1	108
Oatmeal: average, raw	28	1	114
Whitworth's	28	1	115
Porridge Oats: Co-op	28	1	112
Nisa	28	1	110
Whitworth's	28	1	115
Puffed Rice, Tesco	28	1	105
Puffed Wheat: Quaker	28	1	103
Sainsbury	28	1	100
Quick Oats, Tesco	28	1	116
Quick Quaker Oats, Quaker	28	1	105
Rice, brown: boiled	28	1	30
raw	28	1	100
white: boiled	28	1	35
raw	28	1	102
Rice Crunchies, Safeway	28	1	100
Rice Krispies, Kellogg's	28	1	100
Ricicles, Kellogg's	28	1	102
Sago, average, raw	28	1	102

	g	oz	Cal.
Scotch Porridge Oats:			
Sainsbury	28	1	105
Tesco	28	1	115
Semolina, average, raw	28	1	99
Special K, Kellogg's	28	1	100
Sugar Puffs, Quaker	28	1	105
Sultana Bran, Kellogg's	28	1	85
Summer Orchard, Kellogg's	28	1	90
Sunny Grains, Mapleton's	28	1	130
Swiss Style Breakfast:			
Safeway	28	1	110
Sainsbury	28	1	100
Tapioca, average, dry weight	28	1	100
Toasted Bran, Sainsbury	28	1	85
Toasted Farmhouse Bran with Banana & Apple, Weetabix	28	1	96
Weetabix	28	1	100
Weetaflake, Weetabix	28	1	95
Wheat Crunchies, St Michael	28	1	137
Wheatflakes, Energen	28	1	100
Wheat Flakes, Force	28	1	105
Wheatgerm, average	28	1	100

	g	oz	Cal.
Wheat Heart, Holly Mills	28	I	105
Wholewheat Bisks, Sainsbury	each		70
Wholewheat Flakes, Prewetts	28	I	101

CONFECTIONERY

CHOCOLATE BARS

	g	oz	Cal.
Aero, Rowntree Mackintosh:			
milk	bar		210
mini	bar		48
orange	bar		205
peppermint	bar		230
Bar 6, Cadbury	each		220
Big Bar Bandit, McVitie's	each		215
Blue Riband, Rowntree Mackintosh	bar		105
Bounty, Mars, milk or plain	small		136
Bournville Chocolate, Cadbury	28	I	125
Caramac, Rowntree Mackintosh, small	each		165
Chocolate Cream, Fry's	bar		210
Crunchie, Cadbury: small	bar		114
large	bar		193

		g	oz	Cal.
Dairy Crunch Chocolate, Nestlé		32	1¼	161
Drifter, Rowntree Mackintosh	2 pieces			260
Galaxy Milk Chocolate, Mars, small	bar	50	2	240
Ginger Fudge, Carob coated snack, Kalibu	each	35	1¼	145
Golden Cup, Rowntree Mackintosh	small bar			105
Kit Kat, Rowntree Mackintosh	2-finger bar			114
	4-finger bar			247
Lion Bar, Rowntree Mackintosh	each			224
Liqueur Bar, St Michael		28	1	130
Marabou Dime Bar, Barker & Dobson		28	1	135
Marathon Bar, Mars	each			310
Mars Bar		28	1	127
	mini size			90
Milk Chocolate, Nestlé		28	1	150
Milk Chocolate Wafer: Boots	each			345
Terry's	each			175
Milky Bar, Nestlé		28	1	154
Milky Way: Mars	each			135
	mini size			70

		g	oz	Cal.
Nut Milk Chocolate, Nestlé		28	1	150
Orange Cream, St Michael		50	1¾	210
Ovaltine Milk Chocolate, Wander	bar	50	1¾	255
Peppermint Cream, Fry's	small bar			208
Prize, Rowntree Mackintosh	each			225
Star, Cadbury, small	each			270
Taxi, McVitie's	each			90
Toffee Crisp, Rowntree Mackintosh	each			196
Topic, Mars	each			285
Turkish Delight, Fry's	small bar			187
Twix, Mars	twin bar			274
Whole Nut Chocolate, Cadbury	bar	55	2	302
Yorkie, Rowntree Mackintosh:				
almond	each			345
milk	each			355
raisin & biscuit	each			293

CHOCOLATES

After Eights, Rowntree Mackintosh	each			35

		g	oz	Cal.
Chocolate Assortment, Waitrose		28	1	121
Chocolate Coated Brazils, Tesco		28	1	142
Chocolate Coated Peanuts, Tesco		28	1	153
Chocolate Whirls, Cadbury	each			130
Creme Eggs, Cadbury	each			170
Filled chocolates, average		28	1	130
Hazel Whirls, Cadbury		28	1	155
Maltesers, Mars	small bag	38	1½	179
Matchmakers, Rowntree Mackintosh		28	1	140
Milk Chocolate Buttons, Sainsbury		44	1½	210
Milk Chocolate Caramels, Terry's		28	1	132
Milk Chocolate Egg, Sainsbury	each	64	2¼	312
Milk Chocolate Orange Segments, Terry's	each			955
Milk Chocolate Toffee Roll, Callard & Bowser Nuttall	each			35
Milk Tray Assortment, Cadbury		28	1	142
Mini Egg, Cadbury	bag			500

		g	oz	Cal.
Minstrels, Mars	bag			202
Mint Cream: Clarnico's	each			30
Sharps	each			30
Mint Crisps, Elizabeth Shaw	each			30
Neapolitans, Terry's		195	7	856
Old Master Chocolate Liqueurs, Tobler Suchard	box	85	3	360
Orange Chocolate, Callard & Bowser Nuttall	each			30
Orange Crisps, Elizabeth Shaw	each			30
Plain Chocolate Caramels, Terry's		200	7	933
Plain Chocolate Orange, Terry's	whole			945
Praline Eclairs: Fry's		28	1	133
St Michael		28	1	136
Quality Street, Rowntree Mackintosh		28	1	129
Revels, Mars	small bag			175
Rolo, Rowntree Mackintosh	each			24
Roses Chocolate Assortment, Cadbury		28	1	120
Treets, Mars	packet	48	1¾	252

	g	oz	Cal.
Walnut Whip, Rowntree Mackintosh	each		167

HEALTH BARS

	g	oz	Cal.
Alpen Natural Crunch, Weetabix	each		115
Apple & Bran Health, Honeyrose	each		60
Apple & Date Dessert, Prewetts	each		95
Apple, Fruit & Nut, Shepherd Boy	each		150
Apple & Date Health Food, Granose	each		85
Banana Fruit, Prewetts	bar		76
Banana Fruit & Nut Bar, Shepherd Boy	bar		150
Bran & Oat Crunch, Boots	28	1	85
Carob Coated Country, Allinson	bar		151
Carob Coated Sesame, Allinson	bar		105
Carob Fruit, Granose	bar		144
Crunch, Carob Crunch, Kalibu	each		375

		g	oz	Cal.
Crunchy Muesli & Raisin, Bisks	each			40
Crunchy Slice, Holly Mills	bar			187
Date & Fig Dessert, Prewetts	bar			110
Date & Muesli Bar, Boots	bar			155
Fruit, Kalibu		35	1¼	105
Fruit & Bran, Prewetts	bar			85
Fruit, Bran & Honey Crunch Bar, Sainsbury	each			140
Fruit & Nut, Honeyrose	each			100
Fruit & Nut Dessert, Prewetts	bar			130
Fruit & Nut Slice: Holly Mills	each			175
Sunpure	each			175
Ginger Pear, Boots	bar			150
Hazel Carob, Kalibu		42	1½	215
Krunch, Carob Bar, Kalibu		75	2½	375
Mint Carob, Kalibu		28	1	106
	each			313
Nut Muesli, Carob coated, Kalibu	each	35	1¼	140
Oat, Apple & Almond:				
Holly Mills	bar			175
Sunpure	bar			175

	g	oz	Cal.
Oat, Apple & Raisin:			
Holly Mills	bar		165
Sunpure	bar		165
Old Fashioned Honey & Muesli,			
Hornton's	50	2	110
Orange Carob, Kalibu	bar		313
Plain Carob, Kalibu	each		313
Roast Peanut, Holly Mills	each		155
Sesame, Holly Mills	each		135
Sesame Crunch: Allinson	each		115
Planters	each	40	1½	215
Sunflower Fruit & Nut,			
Shepherd Boy	each		190
Wheateats, Allinson	each		89

SWEETS, FUDGE AND GUMS

	g	oz	Cal.
Acid drops	each		20
Barley sugar, average	28	1	100
Boiled sweets, average	28	1	93
Butterscotch: average	28	1	115
boiled, Tesco	28	1	89
Butter Toffee Bon-bons, Fry's	28	1	108
Candy floss, average	stick		60

	g	oz	Cal.
Cough sweet, average: boiled each			10
pastille each			5
Curly Wurly, Cadbury each			130
Dairy Fudge, Sharps each			45
Chocolate Dairy Toffee, Sharps each			45
Dentyne Chewing Gum, all flavours piece			5
Dessert Nougat, Callard & Bowser Nuttall each			55
Devon Toffee, Waitrose	28	1	125
Dolly Mixtures: Bassett's	113	4	440
Sainsbury	113	4	430
St Michael	28	1	110
Double Devon Toffee, St Michael	28	1	125
Doublemint Chewing Gum, Wrigley's each stick			10
Extra Strong Mint, Sharps each			12
Fruit gum, average	28	1	50
Fudge, average	28	1	110
Glacier Fruits, Fox's each			20
Glacier Mints, Fox's each			20
Glees, Mars packet			205

		g	oz	Cal.
Glitter Fruits, boiled, Trebor	each			20
Golden Toffee, Rowntree Mackintosh	each			30
Hacks, all flavours, Fryers		28	1	100
Halva		28	1	125
Hazelnut Toffee Nougat, St Michael		28	1	139
Honey & Lemon, boiled sweets, Trebor	each			20
Hubba Bubba, Wrigley's gum	piece			15
Jelly Babies, Bassett's		28	1	90
Jelly Beans, Sainsbury		28	1	95
Jellytots, Rowntree Mackintosh	packet			155
Jels, Green's	packet			135
Lemon Bon Bon, Sharps toffee	each			25
Lico-Jet, liquorice, Bassett's		28	1	89
Liquorice allsorts, average		28	1	105
Liquorice Comfits, Bassett's		28	1	103
Liquorice Toffee, Callard & Bowser Nuttall	each			39
Liquorice Torpedoes, Bassett's		28	1	103
Little Big Feet, Trebor jellies	each			16

		g	oz	Cal.
Lockets, Mars	small packet			155
Lollyade, Trebor	each			108
Marshmallows: average		28	1	90
Sainsbury		28	1	86
Menthol Stick Pack, Trebor	packet			125
Mini Allsorts, Sainsbury		28	1	105
Mint Butterscotch, Keiller		28	1	110
Mint Lumps, Sainsbury		28	1	136
Mint Imperials, Maynards	bag			400
Mint Imperials, Sainsbury		28	1	95
Mintoes: Callard & Bowser				
Nuttall, loose	each			26
St Michael		28	1	115
Mintola, Rowntree Mackintosh	each			25
Mint Toffee, Callard & Bowser Nuttall, loose	each			38
Mint Toffo, Rowntree Mackintosh	each			20
Murray Mints, Pascall		28	1	114
Nougat, average		28	1	122
Nutty, Rowntree Mackintosh	each			255
Nutty Toffee Puffs, Fry's		28	1	126

	g	oz	Cal.
Opal Sweets, Mars	bag		215
Pacers, Mars	packet		210
Pastilles, St Michael	28	1	96
Peanut Fudge, Callard & Bowser Nuttall	each		220
Pear Drop, Trebor	each		16
Peppermints, average	28	1	110
Pink & White Marshmallows, Barker & Dobson	28	1	110
Polo Fruit, Rowntree Mackintosh	tube		103
Polo Mint, Rowntree Mackintosh	tube		105
Pontefract Cake, Bassett's	113	4	345
Refresher, Trebor	tube		100
Relays, Mars	50	1¾	213
Rock: Edinburgh	stick		101
seaside	stick		90
Rum & Raisin Fudge, Callard & Bowser Nuttall	each		205
Sherbert Bon-bons, Barker & Dobson	28	1	100

	g	oz	Cal.
Smarties, Rowntree Mackintosh fun pack			50
tube			115
Spangles, Mars packet			145
Spearmint Chewing Gum, Wrigley's stick			10
Sugared Almonds, Terry's bag			310
Tigertots, Rowntree Mackintosh bag			175
Toasted Coconut Marshmallows, Barker & Dobson	28	1	108
Toffee Bon Bons, Sharps each			24
Toffees, average	28	1	122
Toffo, Rowntree Mackintosh each			20
Treacle Toffee, Callard & Bowser Nuttall each			40
Tunes, Mars, cherry or honey packet			135
Turkish Delight, Callard & Bowser Nuttall each			35
Tutti Frutti Chews, Trebor each			37
Victory V Gums, Fryers	28	1	86
Victory V Lozenges, Fryers	28	1	95
Yorkshire Recipe Buttermints, Callard & Bowser Nuttall each			31

	g	oz	Cal.
Yorkshire Recipe Treacle Mints, Callard & Bowser Nuttall	each		30
Wine Gums: Bassett's	113	4	352
Fry's	28	1	97

DAIRY PRODUCTS

CHEESE AND CHEESE PRODUCTS

	g	oz	Cal.
Blue brie	28	1	124
Boursin	28	1	115
Brie	28	1	85
Caerphilly	28	1	105
Camembert	28	1	75
Cheddar	28	1	110
Cheddar Slice, Kraft, processed	each		65
Cheesies, Birds Eye	each		60
Cheshire	28	1	110
Cheshire Slice, Kraft, processed	each		65
Cheviot	28	1	119
Cotswold	28	1	105
Cottage, Safeway	carton	113	4	120
Cream, Sainsbury	28	1	125

	g	oz	Cal.
Curd	28	1	35
Danish Blue	28	1	100
Derby	28	1	113
Double Gloucester: with chives & onion, St Ivel	28	1	110
with pickled onion, beer & parsley, St Ivel	28	1	100
Edam	28	1	90
Gorgonzola	28	1	112
Lancashire	28	1	101
Leicester, red	28	1	111
Mozzarella, grated, Sainsbury	28	1	78
Parmesan	28	1	120
Petit Suisse, Sainsbury carton	30	1	42
Philadelphia Full Fat Soft, Kraft	28	1	90
Primula Cheese Spread, plain, Primula	28	1	73
Port Salut	28	1	90
Processed Cheese Slices, Cheddar or Cheshire, Kraft each			65
Quark	28	1	25
Roquefort	28	1	87

	g	oz	Cal.
Stilton	28	1	115
Swiss Knight Processed Gruyère	28	1	90
Tendale, Dairy Crest	28	1	72
Wensleydale	28	1	110
Yarg	28	1	108

EGGS

		g	oz	Cal.
Egg, average	size 1			95
	size 2			90
	size 3			85
	size 4			75
	size 5			70
	size 6			65
Duck egg, average	each	99	3½	170
Quail egg	each			15
Omelette, 3-egg with ham, average	each			250

MILK AND MILK PRODUCTS

		g	oz	Cal.
Butter, average		28	1	220
	1 tablespoon			105
Buttermilk	550ml/1 pint			220
Aerosol Cream, Anchor	1 tablespoon			5

		g	oz	Cal.
Cream, average:	clotted	28	1	165
	Cornish	28	1	153
	double	28	1	128
	single, UHT	28	1	55
	soured	28	1	54
	tinned	28	1	70
	whipped & compressed	28	1	105
	whipping	28	1	105
Milk:	semi-skimmed	600 ml	1 pt	270
	skimmed	600 ml	1 pt	195
	whole	600 ml	1 pt	380
Quark		28	1	25

YOGHURT

		g	oz	Cal.
Apricot, Chambourcy	carton	100	3½	90
Apricot & Passion Fruit, St Michael	carton	100	3½	100
Apricot Mango Tropical, Eden Vale	carton	150	5¼	145
Bonjour, Chambourcy, all fruit flavours	carton	100	3½	85
Diet, Very Low Fat, Yoplait	carton	125	4½	60
Drinking, fresh, Danish Quality Foods, Butterdane		500	17	350
Fruit, average		28	1	30

		g	oz	Cal.
Gooseberry, BhS	carton	150	5¼	175
Greek, Total, strained cow's milk	carton	450	14	608
Harvest Nut Milk, Sainsbury	carton	150	5¼	195
Hazelnut: Co-op	carton	142	5	138
Loseley	carton	140	5	120
Ski	carton	150	5¼	146
Hazelnut, Sainsbury Low Fat	carton	150	5¼	150
Jaffa, Mr Men, Raines	carton	125	4	125
Lebnie, Loseley	carton	280	10	328
Lemon, Chambourcy	carton	125	4½	98
Lemon Fruit, Chambourcy	carton	150	5¼	147
Mandarin, Co-op	carton	142	5	120
Melon & Ginger, Eden Vale	carton	125	4½	157
Melon & Walnut, Chambourcy	carton	100	3½	95
Mr Men, Sainsbury, average	carton	125	4½	125
Muesli, Loseley	carton	125	4½	150
Munch Bunch, strawberry, Eden Vale	carton	125	4½	125
Natural: Cool Country		142	5	110
Eden Vale	carton	150	5¼	90
St Ivel	carton	125	4½	75
St Michael	carton	150	5¼	90

		g	oz	Cal.
Natural Low Fat: Sainsbury	carton	450	14	290
Waitrose	carton	150	5¼	85
Orange, Munch Bunch, Eden Vale	carton	125	4	125
Passion Fruit & Melon, Eden Vale	carton	150	5¼	150
Pasteurised Fruit, Dairytime	carton	150	5¼	75
Pasteurised Natural, Dairytime	carton	150	5¼	145
Peach & Apricot, Sainsbury	carton	150	5¼	120
Peach Melba: BhS	carton	150	5¼	125
Dairytime	carton	120	4½	105
Mr Men	carton	150	5¼	140
Peach & Redcurrant, Chambourcy	carton	142	5	130
Peach, Co-op	carton	142	5	150
Pear & Banana, Dessert Farm	carton	142	5	95
Pear Melba, Ski	carton	150	5¼	135
Pineapple & Coconut, Eden Vale	carton	150	5¼	150
Prize Fruit, St Ivel	carton	142	5	110
Strawberry, Mr Men, Raines	carton	125	4	115
Tropical Fruit, St Michael	carton	150	5¼	156

		g	oz	Cal.
Vanilla, Eden Vale	carton	150	5¼	138
Whole Milk Black Cherry, St Michael	carton	150	5¼	163

DIABETIC

		g	oz	Cal.
Apricot Jam, Country Preserves		28	1	35
Hazelnut Milk Chocolate, Boots		28	1	150
Jelly, Boots	tablet			240
Lemon Curd, Ratcliffe		28	1	95
Milk Chocolate: Boots		28	1	180
Nestlé		28	1	150
Orange Crunch Milk Chocolate, Boots		85	3	460
Pastilles, all flavours, Boots		85	3	90
Plain Chocolate, Boots		85	3	475
Plain Chocolate Shaper Bar, Boots	each			310
Raspberry Jam, Country Preserves		28	1	35
Strawberry Jam, Country Preserves		28	1	35
Threeberry Jam, Country Preserves		28	1	41

DRIED AND GLACÉ FRUIT AND NUTS

		g	oz	Cal.
Almonds:	flaked	1 tablespoon		40
	whole, Princess, Barker & Dobson	28	1	127
Apricots:	average	28	1	52
	Beddingtons Fruit Company	packet 142	4	195
Banana Chips, Tesco		28	1	145
Barcelona nuts, shelled, average		28	1	183
Beechnuts, shelled, average		28	1	160
Big D Tropical Fruit & Nuts, Smiths		packet 50	1¾	175
Brazil Mix, Prewetts		28	1	116
Brazil nuts, average:				
chocolate coated		each		55
shelled		28	1	75
Cashew nuts:	dry roasted	28	1	129
	shelled, plain	28	1	178
Cherry, glacé		28	1	60
Chestnuts:	purée, average	tinned 28	1	65
	shelled	28	1	48

	g	oz	Cal.
Cob nuts: shelled	28	1	28
weighed with shells	28	1	39
Coconut: creamed	28	1	218
desiccated, average	28	1	171
fresh	28	1	102
Currants:, average, dried	28	1	69
Date & Cashew Muesli Tub, Jordans	each		26
Dates: chopped & sugar rolled, average	28	1	77
chopped & sugar rolled, Whitworth's	250	8¾	685
dried, without stone, average	28	1	70
dried, with stone, average	28	1	60
stoned, Whitworth's	250	8¾	620
Doublenut Mix: Granny Smith	packet		820
Lyons Tetley	packet		880
Dry Roasted Peanuts:			
KP	packet	50	2	305
Planters	packet	50	2	285
Sainsbury	packet	113	4	640
Walker's	packet	50	2	265
Figs, average	28	1	60
Ginger stem in syrup, average	28	1	60
Hazelnuts, shelled, average	28	1	108

	g	oz	Cal.
Macedonia nuts, shelled, average	28	1	187
Marrons glacés	28	1	75
Mixed nuts & raisins, average	28	1	151
Mixed peel, candied	28	1	78
Nutmeg			0
Nuts & Raisins, Golden Wonder	28	1	150
Pancho Peanuts, Trebor	each		5
Pancho Raisins, Trebor	each		5
Peach, average	28	1	61
stewed without sugar	28	1	20
Peanuts, average:			
dry roasted	28	1	171
roasted & salted	28	1	162
Peanuts & Raisins, KP	120	4	440
Pear, average	28	1	45
Pecan nuts, average	28	1	150
Pine kernels	28	1	180
Pistachio nuts, weighed with shells, average	28	1	168
Prunes: No-need-to-soak, Whitworth's	375	13	435
uncooked, weighed whole	28	1	38

		g	oz	Cal.
Pumpkin seeds		28	1	180
Raisins, average		28	1	70
Roast Salted Peanuts, KP		25	¾	140
Salted Cashew Nuts, Sainsbury		57	2	320
Salted Peanuts, Golden Wonder	packet			50
Sesame seeds		28	1	168
Sultanas, dried, average		28	1	71
Sunflower seed, skinned		28	1	170
Sweet Peanuts, Trebor	each			25
Tropical Blend Nuts, KP	packet	100	3½	445
Tropical Mix, Whitworth's	packet			205
Walnuts: pickled, Epicure		28	1	20
shelled		28	1	156
with shells		28	1	100
Water Chestnuts, Arnoy	tinned	283	10	104

FATS AND OILS

		g	oz	Cal.
Cod liver oil	1 teaspoon			40
Dripping		28	1	250
	per tablespoon/15ml			125
Flora		28	1	210
Ghee		28	1	235

	g	oz	Cal.
Gold, Standard or Unsalted, St Ivel	28	1	111
Golden Churn Spread, Kraft	28	1	190
Kerrygold Lite Spread, Kerrygold	28	1	110
Lard	28	1	250
Low Fat Spread, Safeway	28	1	100
Margarine, average	28	1	226
Oil per tablespoon/15 ml			125
corn	28	1	255
ground nut	28	1	255
olive	28	1	255
soya bean	28	1	255
sunflower	28	1	255
vegetable	28	1	255
Outline Low Fat Spread, van den Bergh	28	1	105
Shape Low Fat Spread, St Ivel	28	1	112
Slimmers' Spread, Co-op	28	1	105
Suet: block	28	1	255
shredded	28	1	235
dumpling mix, Granny Smith packet			1130
pudding mix, Lyons Tetley packet			1120

	g	oz	Cal.

FISH

	g	oz	Cal.
Bass, average steamed fillet	28	1	35
Bloater, average, grilled, weighed with skin & bones	28	1	53
Catfish, steamed with bones	28	1	28
Caviar, average	28	1	75
Clam, raw without shell	28	1	25
Cockle, boiled without shell	28	1	15
Cod: baked or steamed	28	1	23
fried in batter	28	1	57
Cod's roe	28	1	32
Coley, fillet, steamed	28	1	28
Crab: meat only, boiled	28	1	37
weighed with shell	28	1	7
Prince's	28	1	25
Eel: jellied	28	1	60
raw, flesh only	28	1	50
smoked	28	1	56
Flounder, steamed with bones	28	1	15
Haddock: fried with skin & bones	28	1	21
smoked, steamed with skin & bones	28	1	28
Hake: fried, weighed with skin & bones	28	1	55
steamed, weighed with skin			

	g	oz	Cal.
Halibut, steamed with skin & bones	28	1	28
Herring:			
baked in vinegar, weighed with skin & bones	28	1	50
fried, weighed with skin & bones	28	1	59
roe, raw	28	1	23
John Dory, steamed, weighed with skin & bones	28	1	17
Kipper: grilled or baked	28	1	31
raw	28	1	45
Ling, fried, weighed with skin & bones	28	1	52
Lobster:			
weighed, meat only, cooked	28	1	34
weighed with shell, cooked	28	1	12
Mackerel:			
fried, weighed with skin & bones	28	1	39
kippered, weighed with skin & bones	28	1	70
raw, weighed with skin & bones	28	1	40
smoked, weighed with skin & bones	28	1	68

	g	oz	Cal.
Monkfish:			
fried, weighed with skin & bones	28	1	41
steamed, weighed with skin & bones	28	1	23
Mullet, red or grey, steamed, weighed with skin & bones	28	1	23
Mussels:			
boiled	28	1	25
boiled, weighed with shells	28	1	7
Octopus, raw	28	1	20
Oysters, raw: without shells	28	1	15
with shells	28	1	2
Perch, raw, weighed whole	28	1	35
Pike, raw, weighed whole	28	1	25
Plaice: raw	28	1	26
steamed, weighed with skin & bones	28	1	14
Pollan: fried in oatmeal	28	1	40
steamed, weighed with skin & bones	28	1	16
Pollock, raw, weighed with skin & bones	28	1	25
Prawns: shelled	28	1	30
with shells	28	1	12

	g	oz	Cal.
Saithe: steamed	28	1	28
steamed & weighed whole	28	1	24
Salmon:			
boiled or steamed	28	1	56
boiled or steamed, weighed with skin & bones	28	1	45
raw	28	1	52
smoked	28	1	40
Salmon Trout: raw, flesh only	28	1	50
boiled or steamed	28	1	54
Sardines, raw	28	1	55
Scallops: raw	28	1	20
steamed without shells	28	1	30
Scampi, raw, peeled	28	1	30
Shark, raw, flesh only	28	1	50
Shrimps: fresh, peeled	28	1	33
fresh with shells	28	1	11
drained, average tinned	28	1	27
John West tinned	100	3½	90
Sild in oil, Tesco tinned	110	3¾	300
Skate, fillet, fried in batter	28	1	57
Smelt, boneless, fried	28	1	115

	g	oz	Cal.
Sole, Dover fillet:			
fried	28	1	61
raw	28	1	23
steamed or poached, weighed whole	28	1	18
Sole, lemon, whole, poached	28	1	18
Sprats, fried	28	1	110
Squid, raw	28	1	25
Sturgeon, raw, weighed with bones	28	1	25
Trout, weighed whole:			
poached or grilled	28	1	20
smoked	28	1	21
Turbot, fillet, poached	28	1	28
Whelks, weighed with shells	28	1	4
Whitebait, fried	28	1	152
Whiting:			
fried, weighed whole	28	1	49
smoked fillets, Findus	frozen 28	1	23
steamed, weighed whole	28	1	17
Winkles, steamed or boiled, weighed with shells	28	1	4
Witch:			
fried, weighed whole	28	1	56
steamed, weighed whole	28	1	15

	g	oz	Cal.

FISH DISHES

	g	oz	Cal.
Baked Herrings, Waitrose	28	1	54
Battered Crisp Cod Portions, Birds Eye	28	1	55
Battered Crispy Cod, Ross	28	1	48
Battered Cod Steak, Birds Eye	28	1	64
Breaded Cod Fillet, Bejam, fried	28	1	60
Breaded Cod Steak, Bejam, fried	28	1	50
Buttered Kipper Fillet, Young's	28	1	54
Buttered Smoked Haddock, Young's	100	3½	82
Captain's Pie, Birds Eye	284	10	330
Cod Bake, Ross	28	1	34
Cod in Breadcrumbs, Safeway	28	1	35
Cod with Butter Sauce, Tesco	28	1	21
Cod in Cheese Sauce, Birds Eye	packet		170
Cod Crumble, Ross	28	1	57
Cod Fillet à l'Orange, Findus	packet	280	9½	250
Cod Fish Finger, Birds Eye	each		45
Cod & Prawn Pie, St Michael	28	1	47
Cod Steak in Crisp Crunch Crumbs, Birds Eye	each		180

	g	oz	Cal.
Cod's roe, average, fried in egg & breadcrumbs	28	1	55
Cod Steak in Parsley Sauce, Birds Eye	packet		150
Cod Steak in Seafood Sauce, Birds Eye	packet		155
Crispy Cod Steak, Birds Eye, baked	each		210
Crispy Plaice Fillet, Birds Eye	28	1	60
Curried Prawn Snack Meal, Chambourcy	28	1	40
Dressed Crab, John West	tinned	45	1½	60
Economy Cod Fish Fingers:			
Bejam, grilled	each		57
Findus, grilled	each		45
Fishburger, Birds Eye, baked	each		95
Fish Cake:			
average, fried	28	1	53
average, grilled	each		65
Bejam, grilled without fat	each		115
Findus, grilled	each		60
Fish Finger: average, fried	28	1	65
average, grilled	each		50
Ross, grilled	each		45
Minced Cod, Sainsbury, grilled	each		51

	g	oz	Cal.
Fisherman's Pie: BhS	each		455
St Michael	454	16	615
Fish pie, average	28	1	36
Fish Steak in Butter Sauce, Ross	packet		140
Fish Stick, Ocean Pearl	each		15
Fish & Chips, Wimpy	portion		465
Hake Steaks in Breadcrumbs, Birds Eye	28	1	30
Haddock:			
in batter, Safeway	28	1	57
in Crisp Crunch Crumbs, Birds Eye	each		185
in Crispy Batter, frozen, Bejam	each		212
fillets, breaded and frozen, Waitrose	28	1	40
smoked with butter, Birds Eye	28	1	29
smoked fillet with butter, Ross	packet	170	6	165
Haddock Fish Finger, Findus, grilled	each		54
Haddock Mornay, St Michael	400	14	510
Haddock Steak in Light Crispy Crumb, Findus	packet		250

		g	oz	Cal.
Herring:				
fillets in savoury sauce, John West	tinned	200	7	235
fillets in tomato sauce, John West	tinned	200	7	275
roe, fried		28	1	70
Jumbo Cod Fingers, Ross	each			125
Kedgeree, average		28	1	43
Kipper:				
fillets, boil-in-the-bag, Bejam	packet			380
fillets with butter, Macrae	packet	170	6	370
fillets in oil, Prince's	tinned	190	7	565
fillets, John West	tinned	200	7½	452
Kippered Mackerel Fillets, Macrae	tinned	28	1	55
Mackerel in Brine, Sainsbury	tinned	125	4	250
Mackerel in Oil, Prince's	tinned	125	4	272
Mackerel in Tomato Sauce:				
Prince's	tinned	125	4	195
Shippams	tinned	425	15	764
Ocean Pie: St Michael	packet	227	8	240
Ross	serving	340	9	300
Oven Crispy Cod Steak, Birds Eye				
as sold	each			230
baked or grilled	each			215

	g	oz	Cal.
Oven Crispy Fish Finger, Birds Eye — each			30
Oven Crispy Fish 'n' Chips, Birds Eye — packet			470
Oven Crispy Haddock Steak, Birds Eye:			
as sold — each			230
baked or grilled — each			215
Paella, Vesta, serves 2 — packet			640
Pilchards:			
tinned & drained of oil, average	28	1	54
tinned in tomato sauce, average	28	1	36
tinned in tomato sauce, John West	425	15	550
tinned in tomato sauce, Prince's	227	8	285
tinned in tomato sauce, Shippams	425	15	650
Pink Salmon, John West — tinned	105	3½	142

		g	oz	Cal.
Plaice:				
fillets, breaded, St Michael	packet	454	1 lb	600
fillets in crisp crunch, fried, Birds Eye		190	7	595
fillets, frozen, Waitrose		28	1	38
fried in batter, average		28	1	40
stuffed with ham & cheese, frozen, Bejam		28	1	57
stuffed, St Michael		28	1	33
stuffed with mushrooms, frozen, Bejam		28	1	52
stuffed with prawn & mushroom, Bejam	each			410
whole, battered, grilled, Findus	each			150
Prawn Cocktail Goblet, Mattessons		100	3½	197
Prawn Cocktail Waffles, Safeway		50	1¾	220
Prawn Curry: Chic-o-Roll	packet	170	6	104
Vesta, serves 2	packet			730
Prawn Curry with Rice, Findus	packet			370
Prawn Provençale Noodles, Knorr	tub			215
Prawns, peeled, Armour	tinned	200	7	192
Pressed Cod's Roe, John West	tinned	200	7	210
Red Salmon, John West	tinned	105	3½	210

		g	oz	Cal.
Salmon: average	tinned	28	1	44
red, Sainsbury	tinned	212	7½	165
Salmon Fish Cake:				
fried, average	each			160
grilled without fat, Birds Eye	each			70
Salmon pâté, average		28	1	60
Sardine, tinned:				
in brine, John West	tinned	120	4½	180
in oil drained, average	tinned	28	1	62
in oil, John West	tinned	120	4½	235
in oil, Prince's	tinned	120	4½	415
in tomato sauce, John West	tinned	120	4½	210
Savoury Fish Cake, Birds Eye:				
fried	each			150
grilled without fat	each			65
Scampi: breaded, as sold, Presto		28	1	40
deep-fried, Bejam		28	1	70
Thermidor with Rice,				
Baxters	tinned	312	11	360
Sild in Oil, Gateway	tinned	100	3½	380
Smoked Cod in butter sauce,				
Birds Eye	packet			160
Smoked Haddock with butter,				
Findus	packet	170	6	170
Smoked Haddock Mousse,				
Tesco, fresh	packet			190

		g	oz	Cal.
Smoked Mackerel fillets in oil, drained, John West	tinned	110	4	340
Taramasalata, average		28	1	130
Tuna:				
in brine & drained, average	tinned	28	1	31
in brine, John West	tinned	100	3½	110
in brine, Sainsbury	tinned	198	7	230
in oil & drained, average	tinned	28	1	62
in oil & drained, Prince's	tinned	100	3½	290
Tuna & Mushroom, Tiffany's 'Upper Crust'	pack			1700
Tuna & Vegetables in Curry Sauce, John West	tinned	185	6½	200
Value Cod Fish Finger, frozen, Gateway	each			52
Value Fish Finger, fried, Birds Eye	each			45

FRUIT

	g	oz	Cal.
Apple: baked without sugar	28	1	11
cooking, raw	28	1	11
eating, skin & core	28	1	10
eating, whole, average	28	1	9
stewed with sugar	28	1	18

		g	oz	Cal.
Apricot Halves in Fruit Juice, Sainsbury	tinned	411	14½	125
Apricot:				
raw, fresh, weighed with stones		28	1	7
	each			25
stewed without sugar or stones		28	1	35
stewed with sugar		28	1	19
Banana		28	1	23
Blackberries:				
raw, fresh, frozen		28	1	8
stewed without sugar		28	1	7
Blackcurrants:				
Hartley's	tinned	284	10	170
raw, fresh, frozen, average		28	1	8
stewed without sugar		28	1	7
tinned in syrup		28	1	23
Cherry, average:				
Cocktail	each			10
fresh, weighed with stones		28	1	11
tinned		28	1	20
Cranberries, raw		28	1	4
Damson:				
fresh with stones		28	1	11
Hartley's	tinned	425	15	405
stewed with stones, no sugar		28	1	8
Date, fresh with stone	each	28	1	30

		g	oz	Cal.
Fruit Cocktail:				
Armour	tinned	425	15	405
average	tinned	28	1	26
in apple juice, Koo	tinned	227	8	90
in apple juice, Libby's	tinned	411	14½	325
in apple juice, Waitrose	tinned	205	7	100
Fruit Salad: Del Monte	tinned	227	8	160
John West	tinned	285	10	145
average	tinned	28	1	26
Armour		425	15	405
BhS		150	5¼	310
Ginger stem in syrup, average		28	1	60
Gooseberries:				
green, raw		28	1	5
stewed with sugar		28	1	14
Hartley	tinned	283	10	230
Safeway	tinned	283	10	180
Grapes: black, whole		28	1	14
white, whole		28	1	17
Grapefruit, whole fruit weighed		28	1	3
Grapefruit Segments:				
John West	tinned	285	10	145
Prince's	tinned	285	10	170
Tesco, in natural juices	tinned	538	19	185
Greengage:				
raw		28	1	13

		g	oz	Cal.
stewed with sugar, weighed with stones		28	1	20
Guava: fresh		28	1	16
average	tinned	28	1	17
Kiwi fruit	each			30
Lemon: juice				0
whole		28	1	4
Loganberries:				
fresh		28	1	5
in natural juice, John West	tinned	285	10	105
in syrup, average		28	1	29
Tesco	tinned	411	14½	320
Lychee: fresh	each			8
average	tinned	28	1	19
Mandarin:				
average	tinned	28	1	18
fresh, weighed with skin & pips		28	1	7
in natural juices, John West	tinned	28	1	13
Mandarin Oranges, John West	tinned	298	10½	105
Mango, raw, flesh only		28	1	17
Medlar, weighed whole		28	1	10
Melon: canteloupe, whole		28	1	4
charentais, whole		28	1	3
honeydew, whole		28	1	4
Ogen, whole		28	1	5

		g	oz	Cal.
yellow, whole		28	1	4
seeds		28	1	160
watermelon, whole		28	1	2
Mulberries, raw		28	1	10
Nectarine, weighed with stone		28	1	13
Olives:				
with stones in brine		28	1	23
without stones in brine		28	1	29
stuffed	each			5
Orange: flesh		28	1	10
skin, pips		28	1	7½
weighed with skin		28	1	7
whole fruit, small		140	5	35
Passion fruit, weighed whole		28	1	4
Paw-Paw, fresh, flesh only		28	1	11
	tinned	28	1	19
Peach:				
fresh, weighed with stone		28	1	9
tinned, in natural juices, average		28	1	13
tinned, in syrup, average		28	1	25
Prince's	tinned	411	14½	360
Peach Halves or Slices in fruit juice, Del Monte	tinned	411	14½	192
Peach Slices in apple juice, Sainsbury	tinned	411	14½	145

		g	oz	Cal.
Pear:				
in apple juice, Waitrose	tinned	205	7	100
in natural juice, average	tinned	28	1	11
raw, weighed whole		28	1	9
in syrup, average		28	1	22
in syrup, Safeway	tinned	411	15	315
stewed, without sugar		28	1	8
Pear Halves:				
in apple juice, Koo	tinned	227	8	103
Del Monte	tinned	227	8	108
Pear Quarters in Natural Juice,				
John West	tinned	285	10	145
Pineapple:				
fresh, weighed without skin		28	1	13
in natural juice, average	tinned	28	1	15
in syrup, average	tinned	28	1	22
Pineapple Slices:				
in syrup, Del Monte	tinned	234	8	185
in natural juice, Sainsbury	tinned	227	8	105
Pineapple Titbits, Libby's	tinned	411	14½	237
Plum:				
cooking, weighed with stones		28	1	7
Smedley's	tinned	540	19	430
Victoria, weighed with stones		28	1	10
Pomegranate: flesh only		28	1	20
juice		28	1	13

		g	oz	Cal.
Prune:				
Hartley's	tinned	210	7½	205
ready cooked, Whitworth's	dried	28	1	35
stewed without sugar, weighed whole		28	1	19
in natural juice, Safeway	tinned	220	7½	250
Pumpkin, raw, flesh only		28	1	4
Quinces		28	1	7
Raspberries:				
average		28	1	7
average	tinned	28	1	25
in juice, Co-op	tinned	220	7½	65
in syrup, Sainsbury		213	7	184
Redcurrants:				
raw		28	1	6
stewed without sugar		28	1	4
Rhubarb:				
Sainsbury	tinned	538	19	162
stewed without sugar		28	1	2
Satsuma	each	70	2½	20
Strawberries:				
fresh		28	1	7
Fruit Fruitfull, Beddington's	packet	142	5	180
Hartley's	tinned	284	10	325
in syrup, Safeway	tinned	312	11	185
in syrup, Sainsbury	tinned	370	13	250
drained, average	tinned	28	1	23

	g	oz	Cal.
Tangerine, weighed whole	28	1	9
White currants, stewed without sugar	28	1	6

HERBS, SPICES AND BASICS

		g	oz	Cal.
Arrowroot		28	1	100
Bovril Cubes	each			10
Brown Sugar Teamates, Patersons	each			60
Caper		28	1	5
Carob powder		28	1	50
Chilli: dried		28	1	85
fresh		28	1	6
Chive		28	1	10
Curry paste, average		28	1	42
Curry powder, average		28	1	66
Gelatine		28	1	95
Ginger: ground		28	1	72
root, peeled		28	1	18
Glucose, liquid, BP		28	1	90

	g	oz	Cal.
Grenadine syrup	28	1	72
Gherkin	28	1	5
Horseradish:			
creamed, Gateway	28	1	47
hot, Burgess	28	1	58
raw	28	1	17
relish, Colman	28	1	28
Hot Chilli Sauce, Sharwood	28	1	39
Humus, average	28	1	50
Lentils: brown, boiled	28	1	32
brown, uncooked	28	1	104
red, boiled	28	1	28
red, uncooked	28	1	86
Malt extract, average	28	1	86
Marmite	28	1	2
Mild Curry Paste, Sharwood	28	1	57
Mint Jelly, Pearce Duff	28	1	74
Mustard Powder:			
average	28	1	132
Colmans made up	28	1	50
Natex Low Salt Savoury Spread, Modern Health Products	28	1	60
Nutmeg			0

		g	oz	Cal.
Olive:	with stone in brine	28	1	23
	without stone in brine	28	1	29
	stuffed	each		5
	stuffed, Crosse & Blackwell	28	1	15
Oxo Cube, average		each		10
Pepper, all kinds				0
Pumpkin seeds		28	1	180
Salt				0
Sesame seeds		28	1	168
Sugar:	brown, caster, Demerara, granulated, icing & white	28	1	112
	lump: large	each		20
	small	each		10
Sunflower seeds, skinned		28	1	170
Tomato Purée:	average	28	1	20
	Buitoni	tube		94
Vanilla essence		28	1	0
Vegetable Cube, Knorr Stock Cube		each		35
Vindaloo Curry Sauce, Sharwood's Goan		tinned	283	10	220
Vinegar		1 tablespoon		½

	g	oz	Cal.
Virol	28	1	99
Yeast Extract, Natex	28	1	70
Yeast: dried	28	1	48
fresh	28	1	15

JAMS, PRESERVES AND PICKLES

	g	oz	Cal.
Beetroot Pickle:			
Baxter's	28	1	10
Epicure, sweet, sliced	28	1	13
Beetroot & Redcurrant Relish, Baxter's	28	1	48
Branston Pickle, Crosse & Blackwell	28	1	43
Chutney:			
average, apple	28	1	57
average, tomato	28	1	43
average, mango	28	1	120
mango, Burgess	28	1	60
mango & ginger, Green Label, Sharwood	28	1	60
peach, Sharwood	28	1	50
Extra Jams, all flavours, Chivers	28	1	71
Honey, average	28	1	90

FOOD

	g	oz	Cal.
Honeycomb	28	1	80
Jam, average:			
made with edible seeds	28	1	60
made with stone fruit	28	1	60
Lemon Cheese, Hartley's	28	1	85
Lemon Curd: average	28	1	80
Chivers	28	1	80
Gales	28	1	79
Mango Chutney, Pan-Yan	28	1	62
Marmalade:			
average, home-made	28	1	74
Country Basket, no sugar	28	1	32
Frank Cooper Oxford			
Coarse Cut	28	1	75
Roses	28	1	75
Mayonnaise: average	28	1	205
Burgess	28	1	172
Hellmann's	28	1	172
Mild Chilli Relish, Bicks	28	1	26
Mixed Pickles, Haywards	28	1	2
Mustard Piccalilli, Asda	28	1	13
Piccalilli:			
Hayward's	28	1	8
Heinz, Ploughmans	28	1	20

	g	oz	Cal.
Pickled Silverskin Onions:			
average	each		5
Epicure	28	1	4
Sweet, Epicure	28	1	7
Pickled Gherkins, Epicure	28	1	5
Pickled Sliced Beetroot, Epicure	28	1	15
Pickled Walnuts, Epicure	28	1	22
Ploughmans Pickle, Heinz	28	1	34
Sweetcorn Relish, Presto	28	1	32
Sweet Military Pickle, Hayward's	28	1	37
Sweet Pickle, Happy Farm	28	1	38
Sweet Pickled Onions, Co-op	28	1	45
Tomato & Chilli Relish, Sainsbury	28	1	31
Tomato & Pepper Relish, Crosse & Blackwell	28	1	34
Tomato Chutney, Baxter's	28	1	46
Tomato Relish, Burgess	28	1	31
Wild Bramble Jelly, Baxter's	28	1	74

	g	oz	Cal.

MEAT

		g	oz	Cal.
Bacon:				
collar joint, boiled, lean & fat		28	1	92
grilled well, average	rasher	30–35	1–1¼	80
streaky, grilled or fried	rasher	20	¾	50
Beef:				
brisket, boiled		28	1	90
fillet steak, grilled		175	6	250
minced beef, raw		28	1	65
minced beef, fried in oil, drained of fat		28	1	80
rump steak: fried & trimmed		28	1	54
well grilled, raw weight		175	6	260
grilled rare, raw weight		175	6	310
silverside, boiled		28	1	69
sirloin, roasted		28	1	80
stewing steak: braised		28	1	65
raw		28	1	50
topside: raw		28	1	53
roasted		28	1	62
Brains: calf's, boiled		28	1	43
lamb's, boiled		28	1	36
Brawn		28	1	43
Gammon, boiled:				
lean & fat		28	1	91
lean only		28	1	54

	g	oz	Cal.
Gammon rashers:			
fried: back, lean & fat	28	1	121
streaky, lean & fat	28	1	138
grilled: back, lean & fat	28	1	113
streaky, lean & fat	28	1	118
Hare: roast	28	1	55
stewed or baked	28	1	54
Heart, sheep's	28	1	68
Kidney: ox, stewed	28	1	45
sheep, fried	28	1	33
Lamb:			
leg: lean & fat without bone	28	1	68
roast, lean & fat without bone	28	1	75
loin chop, grilled, average size			160
stewing, lean & fat without bone	28	1	72
Liver:			
calf's: fried	28	1	72
uncooked	28	1	43
chicken: fried	28	1	55
uncooked	28	1	38
lamb's: fried	28	1	66
raw	28	1	51
ox, stewed	28	1	55
pig's, raw	28	1	44
Oxtail:			
stewed & weighed with bones	28	1	25
stewed & weighed without bones	28	1	70

	g	oz	Cal.
Ox tongue, boiled & pressed	28	1	35
Pork:			
chop, grilled, lean & fat, weighed whole	28	1	73
leg, roast, lean & fat	28	1	90
loin, roast, lean only	28	1	81
shoulder, St Michael chilled meats	28	1	36
Rabbit, stewed, weighed with bones	28	1	26
Silverside, Mattessons	28	1	50
Snails	28	1	25
Sweetbreads, lamb: fried	28	1	65
raw	28	1	37
Tripe, stewed	28	1	28
Veal: fillet, roast	28	1	65
escalope, fried	28	1	61
Venison, roast	28	1	56

MEAT DISHES

	g	oz	Cal.
Beef Chow Mein, Batchelor's Snack Pot	28	1	205
Beef Curry, Vesta, cooked 2-serving packet			945

	g	oz	Cal.
Beef Curry with Rice, Birds Eye Menu Master packet			380
Beef & Gravy, Batchelor's tin			495
Beef Grill Steak, Ross each			284
Beef & Kidney, Batchelor's tinned			392
Beef & Onion, Tesco	198	7	278
Beef Loaf, Safeway	680	24	1925
Beef Stew, Campbells tinned	425	15	270
Beef Stew & Dumplings, Birds Eye Menu Master packet			320
Boeuf Bourguignon, Baxters tinned	440	15½	440
Boiled Beef & Carrots, Ross 1 meal			250
Breaded Beef Grill, Safeway each			340
Chilli Beef Grillado, Findus each			160
Corn Beef Hash: Tiffany tin			185
Sharwoods each			168
Cottage pie, average	28	1	89
Dinner Balls, Granose tinned	100	3½	145
Doner kebab, average each			550
Faggots:			
average	28	1	75
Birds Eye, in rich sauce	369	13	690
Brains, in rich sauce each			120

		g	oz	Cal.
Faggots with onions in rich sauce, Ross		100	3½	160
Gammon-Style Turkey Steak, grilled, Matthew's		28	1	105
Gravy & Lean Roast Beef, Birds Eye	packet			95
Hash Browns, frozen, Ross		28	1	23
Haggis, cooked, average		28	1	88
Hot Dogs, Wall's, tinned	each			60
Hot Dogs, mini, Tesco	tinned	28	1	60
International Grill, Wimpy	portion			730
Irish Stew: Newforge	tinned	400	14	255
Tyne Brand	tinned	392	14	375
Kashmir Beef Curry, Knorr	tub			195
Lamb Casserole, Ross		100	3½	100
Lamb Dalesteak, grilled, Dale Pak		85	3	200
Liver with Onion & Gravy, Birds Eye Menu Master Meal	pack			190
London Grill, Crosse & Blackwell Ready Meal		283	10	445
Meatballs: Danepak, fresh	each			32
in curry sauce, Campbells		425	15	485

		g	oz	Cal.
in gravy, Campbells		425	15	450
in tomato sauce, Campbells		425	15	408
Mince, Baxters, Scotch		432	15½	425
Mince Bolognese, Tyne Brand	tinned	412	14½	490
Minced Beef & Onion in gravy, Co-op	tinned	425	15	690
Minced Beef Savoury Toast, Findus, warmed	each			140
Minced Beef & Vegetables, Ross	each			400
Nut Brawn, Granose	tinned	284	10	600
Pork & Apple Casserole, frozen, Ross	packet			220
Pork & Beef Sausage, Cotswold Style	each			120
Pork Dalesteak, Dale Pak, well grilled	each			180
Roast Beef Dinner, Birds Eye, frozen	tray			357
Roast Beef in Gravy, Findus		100	3½	100
Rogan Gosht: Chic-o-Roll	packet	170	6	150
Home Pride	tinned			380
Sausage: beef: chipolata, well grilled	each			50
large, well grilled	each			120

		g	oz	Cal.
skinless, well grilled	each			65
Waitrose		28	1	82
pork: Bejam, thick, well grilled	each			160
boiling ring		28	1	110
chipolata, well grilled	each			65
large, well grilled	each			125
skinless, well grilled	each			95
Wall's Thick		28	1	105
pork & beef: chipolata, well grilled	each			60
large, well grilled	each			125
turkey & pork: Matthew's, grilled	each			160
Sausage meat, uncooked		28	1	80
Savoury Pudding, Granose	tinned	454	16	940
Savoury Soufflé, Daloon	pack			610
Shepherd's pie		100	3½	250
Spare Ribs in Barbecue Sauce:				
Chic-o-Roll		227	8	410
Mr Chang	packet	227	8	420
Stewpot, Ross, Beef & Kidney	each			495
Sweet & Sour Pork with Rice, Birds Eye	packet			670
Sweet & Sour Pork with Vegetables, Uncle Wong's		283	10	440

	g	oz	Cal.
Toad-in-the-hole, average	225	8	500
Wimpy Grill, Wimpy	each		218

DELICATESSEN

		g	oz	Cal.
Ardennes Pâté, Mattessons		28	1	100
Black Pudding:				
average, sliced and fried		28	1	85
Mattessons		28	1	102
Bavarian Ham Sausage, St Michael		28	1	46
Bierwurst, St Michael		28	1	57
Bratwurst, Mattessons		28	1	95
Bridie Meatloaf, Safeway		28	1	82
Chopped Pork & Ham, Mattessons		28	1	94
Corned Beef, Fray Bentos	tinned	28	1	62
Cured Pork Shoulder, St Michael		28	1	27
Cured Salt Beef, St Michael		28	1	47
Danish Salami: Chic-o-Roll		28	1	140
Sainsbury		28	1	165
Dutch Smoked Pork Sausage, Sainsbury		28	1	90

	g	oz	Cal.
Farmhouse Beef & Onion Slice, Kraft	113	4	415
Farmers Slice, Wall's	283	10	900
Frankfurter: Mattessons	28	1	100
Sainsbury	28	1	70
French Garlic Sausage:			
Co-op	28	1	75
Sainsbury	28	1	55
Tesco	28	1	80
Garlic Sausage, Bowyers	28	1	85
German Cervelat Sausage, Sainsbury	28	1	120
German Salami, Sainsbury	28	1	95
German Sausage, Mattessons	28	1	70
German Style Sausage, Wall's	28	1	69
Grosvenor Pork Pie, Wall's	113	4	410
Ham:			
Parma, St Michael	28	1	85
honey roasted, St Michael	28	1	62
Virginia, Co-op	28	1	35
York, boiled, lean only	28	1	62
Ham Sausage, Mattessons	28	1	38
Haslet, average	28	1	80

		g	oz	Cal.
Liver Sausage: average		28	1	88
Bowyers		28	1	60
Lunch Tongue, Mattessons		28	1	75
Luncheon Meat: average		28	1	89
Wall's	tinned	340	12	1140
Luncheon sausage, average		28	1	80
Parma Ham, St Michael		28	1	85
Pâté:				
Brussels, Mattesons		28	1	117
chicken, Mattessons		28	1	72
crab spreading, Prince's		28	1	82
ham & tongue, Mattessons		28	1	60
liver, Wall's	tinned	150	5¼	436
liver & bacon, Mattessons		28	1	86
liver & ham, Mattessons		28	1	85
smoked, Prince's	tinned	28	1	42
vegetable, Granose	tinned	114	4	333
Polony, Mattessons		28	1	57
Pork Breakfast Sausage, Sainsbury		28	1	75
Pork Luncheon Meat:				
Armour	tinned	340	12	1040
Mattessons		28	1	92
Sainsbury, barbecue flavour		28	1	58
Pork & Pepper Loaf, Mattessons		28	1	70
Pork Pie, Bowyers	medium size			74

	g	oz	Cal.
Salami:			
Belgian	28	1	130
Danish	28	1	160
Danish, Sainsbury	28	1	165
German	28	1	120
Hungarian	28	1	130
Hungarian, Sainsbury	28	1	140
Italian, St Michael	28	1	140
Salmon Trout Fish Pâté, Faroe	pack		230
Sausage:			
Belgian liver	28	1	90
bierwurst	28	1	75
bockwurst	28	1	180
cervelat	28	1	140
chorizo	28	1	140
continental liver	28	1	80
French garlic	28	1	90
garlic	28	1	70
German Garlic, Sainsbury	28	1	95
ham	28	1	50
kabanos	28	1	115
krajana, Sainsbury	28	1	35
krakowska	28	1	80
mettwurst	28	1	120
mortadella	28	1	105
pastrami	28	1	65
Polish	28	1	60
polony	28	1	80
smoked	28	1	130

	g	oz	Cal.
Sausage Roll: Bowyers	70	2	285
Bowyers, jumbo	125	4	430
Sainsbury, mini	each		100
Scotch Eggs: Bowyers	each		350
Tesco	each		330
Stuffed Pork Roll, Bowyers	28	1	90
Tongue: lamb's, stewed	28	1	82
ox, boiled	28	1	83
Turkey & Ham Roll, Wall's	tinned 200	7	480
Turkey Meat Loaf, Buxted	28	1	62

PANCAKES, SAVOURY

	g	oz	Cal.
Chicken & Bacon, Findus	each		100
Chicken with Mushroom Crêpes, Findus	28	1	38
Chicken & Mushroom, Birds Eye	each		110
Minced Beef, Findus	each		105
Scotch, Sainsbury	each		70
Vegetable Crêpes, Sainsbury	340	12	340
Wholemeal Mix, Quaker	28	1	105

	g	oz	Cal.

PANCAKES, SWEET

		g	oz	Cal.
Buttermilk mix, Quaker		28	1	130
Hazelnut Pancake Mix, Quaker Mix	packet			110
Ice Cream, Daloon	each			110
Syrup & Sultana, Sunblest	each			85

PASTA AND PIZZAS

		g	oz	Cal.
Alphabetti Spaghetti with tomato sauce, Crosse & Blackwell		213	7½	130
Cannelloni: Buitoni	tinned	400	14	388
Findus	frozen	350	12¼	435
Capricciosa Pizza, Pizza Express	each			885
Cheese & Tomato Pizza, Safeway	each	180	6½	380
Cheesey Pasta, Kraft		28	1	48
Four Seasons Pizza, Pizza Express	each			890
French Bread Pizza:				
BhS	each			310
Findus, Cheese	each	142	5	290
Ross	each			300

		g	oz	Cal.
Ham & Mushroom Pizza, Birds Eye	each	265	9¼	640
Ham & Pineapple Pizza, Findus	each	170	6	320
Italian Pizza, Iceland	each			983
Lasagne:				
Birds Eye Menu Master Meal	frozen	250	8¾	317
Findus	frozen	283	10	340
St Michael	frozen	283	10	380
Long Spaghetti in sauce, Nisa	tinned	220	7¾	145
Macaroni:				
boiled		28	1	32
wholewheat, boiled, plain		28	1	32
wholewheat, raw		28	1	92
Macaroni Cheese: average		28	1	59
Iceland	packet			290
Safeway	tinned	210	7½	250
Margherita Pizza, Pizza Express	each			770
Marinara Pizza, Pizza Express	each			700
Mushroom Pasta Menu, Crosse & Blackwell	packet			103
Mushroom Pizza, Marietta's	17.5cm(7in)			520
Mushroom Pizza, Pizza Express	each			700
Napoletana Pizza, Pizza Express	each			810

	g	oz	Cal.
Noodles: cooked	28	1	34
raw	28	1	102
Noodle Doodles, Heinz tinned	215	7½	120
Party Pizza, Sainsbury, family size each			1010
Pepperoni, Cheese & Tomato Pizza, St Michael each	518	18	1055
Pizza Base Mix, Granny Smith packet			500
Pizza Deluxe, Birds Eye each			360
Pizza Fingers, Marietta's each			95
Pizza Pie, McVitie's each			440
Pizza Prima, BhS each			700
Pizza, Tomato & Cheese, Ross 12cm(5in)			240
Pot Noodles, Beef & Tomato, Golden Wonder pot			385
Ravioli, Buitoni tinned	200	7	145
Ravioli in Tomato Sauce, Heinz tinned	215	7½	145
Savoury Barbecue Beef Pizza, Findus each			400
Seafood Fettucine, St Michael frozen	350	12	650
Spaghetti:			
boiled, plain	28	1	33
raw	28	1	107

	g	oz	Cal.
tinned in tomato sauce	28	1	17
wholewheat, raw	28	1	97
Spaghetti Alphabet with Tomato Sauce, Crosse & Blackwell	213	7½	130
Spaghetti Hoops in Tomato Sauce, Heinz	215	7½	145
Spaghetti Rings in Tomato Sauce, Crosse & Blackwell	213	7½	130
Special Pizza, Marietta's	17cm(7in)		610
Spicy Curry, Golden Wonder Pot Noodles with Sauce	pot		315
Taco Shell, Old El Paso	each		50
Tagliatelli, Rossi	400	14	690
Tagliatelli with Mushrooms & Ham, Sainsbury	packet 560	20	1160
Tomato, Cheese & Ham Pizza, St Michael	each 454	16	970
Tomato & Cheese Party Pizza, BhS	each		260
Tomato & Cheese Pizza Snack:			
Birds Eye	93	3¼	145
Marietta's	12cm(5in)		210
Tortellini, Pasta Reale	28	1	83

FOOD

		g	oz	Cal.
Traditional Cannelloni, McVitie's	packet	350	12½	420
Wholewheat Pasta, Record		100	3½	327
Veneziana Pizza, Pizza Express	each			750

PASTRY AND BATTER

		g	oz	Cal.
Pastry:				
choux:	baked	28	1	95
	raw	28	1	60
flaky:	baked	28	1	150
	raw	28	1	115
puff:	baked	28	1	115
	Birds Eye	28	1	120
	Jus-Rol	28	1	114
	raw	28	1	115
	Ploughman's, Kraft	142	5	433
shortcrust:	baked	28	1	150
	Birds Eye	28	1	125
	Jus-Rol	28	1	125
	Safeway	28	1	122
	raw	28	1	130
wholemeal:	baked	28	1	145
	raw	28	1	120
Pastry Mix, Lyons		28	1	133
Quick Batter Mix, Whitworth's	packet	500	17½	1690
Traditional Pastry, Freshbake		149	5¼	460

	g	oz	Cal.
Vol-au-Vent Pastry Case, Jus-Rol:			
cocktail size			40
medium size			72
Yorkshire Pudding: average	28	1	60
Jus-Rol	each		30
Viota mix	each		492
Yorkshire Pudding & Pancake			
Mix, Whitworth's	255	9	889

PIES, PIE FILLINGS, FLANS AND QUICHES

SAVOURY

	g	oz	Cal.
Bacon & Cheese Flan, Sainsbury	each		380
Beef Pie, Birds Eye Value	each		370
Beef Steak Pie, Brains	each		1232
Beef & Vegetable Pie with			
Onion, St Michael, hot	28	1	61
Cheese, Egg & Bacon Flan:			
Birds Eye	28	1	92
St Michael	28	1	73
Chicken & Mushroom Pie:			
Birds Eye	each		360
Fray Bentos	28	1	56

		g	oz	Cal.
Chicken & Vegetable Pie, Findus		28	1	54
Egg, Cheese & Bacon Flan, Findus	each	450	16	970
Gala Pie, Bowyers		115	4	365
Lattice Pork Pie, Tesco		28	1	111
Luxury Smoked Ham & Cheese Quiche, Sainsbury		28	1	67
Luxury Spanish Quiche, Sainsbury		28	1	67
Meat & Potato Pie, Freshbake		113	4	350
Melton Mowbray Pie, Sainsbury	each	283	10	970
Melton Mowbray Pork Pie, Wall's	each			610
Minced Beef Pie, Wall's family size	each			1090
Minced Beef & Vegetable Pie, Birds Eye	each			409
Minced Pork Pie, Sainsbury		142	5	470
Minced Steak & Onion Pie Filling, Fray Bentos	tinned	425	15	840
Natural Pork Pie, Sainsbury		128	4½	472
Party Pork Pie, Wall's	each			1010

		g	oz	Cal.
Pork Pie:	average	28	1	104
	Bowyers, individual	140	5	550
	Wall's	142	5	585
Potato, Cheese & Bacon Flan, Sainsbury		170	6	360
Premium Steak Pie, Sainsbury		142	5	360
Raised Pork Pie:	Bowyers	530	19	1890
	Wall's	454	16	1747
Salmon & Broccoli Flan, Sainsbury	each			1020
Scotch Pie, Wall's		113	4	320
Shepherd's Pie, Birds Eye		27	8	270
Steak & Kidney Pie:	Birds Eye	each		370
	BhS	152	5½	385
Steak & Kidney Pudding, Fray Bentos	tin	213	7½	465
Steak & Mushroom Pie Filling, Fray Bentos		425	15	615
Steak & Onion Pie Filling, Fray Bentos		425	15	670
Turkey Pie, BhS	each			1250
Turkey in Rich Pastry, St Michael		28	1	90

		g	oz	Cal.
Vegetable & Steak Pie, Fray Bentos	tinned	213	7½	390
Vegetable & Steak Pie Filling, Fray Bentos	tinned	425	15	622

PIES, PIE FILLINGS, FLANS AND QUICHES

SWEET

		g	oz	Cal.
Apple & Blackberry, Batchelor's Pack A Pie	jar	405	14¼	350
Apple & Blackberry Fruit Pie Filling, Mortons	tinned	385	13½	255
Apple & Raspberry, Batchelor's Pack A Pie	jar	405	14¼	350
Apple & Raspberry Fruit Pie Filling, Pickerings	tinned	385	13½	255
Apricot Pie Filling, Sainsbury		397	14	355
Gooseberry Flan Filling, Armour	tin	850	30	755
Harvest Pie, Lyons:				
apple	each			355
apple & blackcurrant	each			354

		g	oz	Cal.
Lemon Pie Filling:				
Birds Eye, made up	packet			255
Royal, made up	packet			490
Mincemeat: average		28	1	37
Hartley's		28	1	86
Mince Pie: average		28	1	111
Mr Kipling	each			204
Pineapple Flan Filling, Armour	tinned	850	30	835
Plum, Batchelor's Pack A Pie		405	14¼	242
Raspberry Flan Filling, Armour	tinned	250	9	1005
Raspberry Fruit Pie Filling, Sainsbury	tinned	397	14	420
Red Cherry Pie Filling, Co-op	tinned	400	14	310
Redcurrant & Raspberry, Batchelor's Pack A Pie	jar			300
Redcurrant & Raspberry Pie, Mr Kipling	each			192
Strawberry Flan Filling, Armour	tin	850	30	1105
Strawberry Fruit Pie Filling:				
Pickering's		395	14	290
Sainsbury		397	14	490
Swiss Black Cherry Fruit Pie Filling, Sainsbury		397	14	395

	g	oz	Cal.

POULTRY

	g	oz	Cal.
Chicken:			
breast, fried, weighed with skin & bone	175	6	215
breast, grilled, weighed with skin & bone	175	6	200
drumstick, fried in egg & breadcrumbs, raw weight	85	3	130
meat, boiled	28	1	52
Duck:			
leg portion, baked:			
meat only	28	1	120
meat & skin	28	1	165
raw: meat only	28	1	35
meat, fat & skin	28	1	122
roast: meat only	28	1	54
meat, fat & skin	28	1	96
wing, baked: meat only	28	1	55
meat & skin	28	1	55
Goose, roast, meat only	28	1	90
Grouse, weighed with bones	28	1	32
Guinea fowl, roast & on the bone	28	1	30
Partridge: meat only	28	1	60
roast, weighed with bones	28	1	37

		g	oz	Cal.
Pheasant: roast, weighed whole		28	1	29
roast, meat only		28	1	64
Pigeon, roast, weighed whole		28	1	29
Quail, roast, weighed whole		100	3½	90
Turkey, roast, weighed with skin & stuffing		28	1	52

POULTRY DISHES

		g	oz	Cal.
Chicken Battercrisp, St Michael		28	1	69
Chicken Chow Mein, St Michael	packet	283	10	230
Chicken in a bun, Wimpy	each			530
Chicken in Jelly, St Michael	tinned	28	1	51
Chicken Kiev, St Michael	packet	312	11	820
Chicken Korma, St Michael	packet	397	14	1050
Chicken & Mushroom Casserole, Birds Eye Menu Master	packet			160
Chicken Supreme, Beanfeast		28	1	84
Chicken in White Sauce, Tesco	tinned	28	1	71
Chicklets, Birds Eye	each			130
Duck in orange sauce, average				600

	g	oz	Cal.
Goldenbake Chicken Portions, ovenbaked, Bejam, Southern Style	28	1	85
Golden Chicken with Noodles, Heinz Super Mugs	tub		70
Imperial Chicken & Fried Rice, Uncle Wong	320	11½	445
Roast Breast of Chicken, St Michael	28	1	60
Sweet & Sour Chicken, Vesta 2-serving packet			1020
Tandoori Flavour Chicken, St Michael	28	1	75
Tandoori Flavour Chicken Quarters, Bejam frozen	28	1	75

PUDDINGS

	g	oz	Cal.
Angel Delight, Bird's:			
Butterscotch, made up with skimmed milk packet			415
Banana, made up with whole milk packet			440
Chocolate, made up with skimmed milk packet			332
Wild Strawberry, made up with whole milk packet			440

	g	oz	Cal.
Apple & Blackberry Crumble, Tiffany's — each			1080
Apple & Blackcurrant Pie, Lyons mini size			175
Apple Cream Dessert, St Michael	28	1	48
Apple crumble, average	28	1	57
Apple Pie: Freshbake, family size — each	454	16	1170
Lyons, mini size — each			175
Lyons, Harvest Pie Dessert — each			1025
McDonald's — each			250
Wimpy — each			315
Baked Alaska, Mary Baker Simply Sweet, Nabisco Frear — packet			990
Baked Jam Roll, St Michael	28	1	111
Bakewell Tart, Mr Kipling — each			1245
Bakewell Tarts, Green's — packet			1290
Banana Long Boat, Wimpy — each			280
Blackcurrant Pie, Waitrose	28	1	99
Blackcurrant Yoghurt Cheesecake, Green's — packet			1095

	g	oz	Cal.
Blancmange, Brown & Polson:			
chocolate, not made up	1 pint sachet		136
vanilla, not made up	1 pint sachet		120
all other flavours not made up	1 pint sachet		125
Blueberry Muffin, Betty Crocker	packet		1440
Canary pudding, average	28	1	131
Caramel Supreme, Eden Vale	carton		158
Castle pudding, average	28	1	112
Chocolate Layer Cake, St Michael	28	1	95
Chocolate Seville, Eden Vale	carton		115
Chocolate Supreme, Eden Vale	carton		170
Chocolate Nut Sundae, Wimpy	each		230
Creamed Rice, Ambrosia	tinned 439	15½	394
Creamed Rice, Waitrose	tinned 440	15½	385
Creme Caramel, Eden Vale	28	1	42
Custard: with cream added	28	1	56
powder	28	1	100
powder made up to 150ml (¼ pint) with skimmed milk			130
Custard tart, average	28	1	82
Egg Custard Tart, St Michael	each		215
Egg Custard Powder, Green's	54	2	620

PUDDINGS

		g	oz	Cal.
Flanby Caramel, Chambourcy	carton			108
Flan Case, Lyons	each			480
Fresh Fruit Salad without cream, Pizza Express	portion			82
Fruit & Nut Sundae, Wimpy	portion			235
Dairy Custard, Co-op		425	15	500
Date Dessert, Whitworth's	tub			425
Dessert Mix, Boots: banana, butterscotch, chocolate, peach or strawberry, made up with whole milk	per serving			65
Devon Custard, Ambrosia		439	15½	440
snack size		170	6	175
Devonshire Individual Trifle, Ross, all flavours	each			170
Fruit Cocktail Trifle, St Ivel	carton			160
Gooseberry Crumble, Tiffany's	each			1040
Instant Custard, Brown & Polson	sachet			355
Instant Whip, Bird's: banana, peach, strawberry, vanilla	packet			525
chocolate	packet			510
butterscotch, toffee	packet			528

		g	oz	Cal.
Jam roll, baked, average		28	1	115
Jam Roly Poly, Tiffany's	each			1045
Jam Tarts: average		28	1	42
Lyons	each			100
Jelly: Chivers, all flavours	block			285
	cube			30
made up with milk		28	1	25
made up with water		28	1	16
Rowntree, all flavours	block	135	4½	350
	cube			30
Leicester pudding, average		28	1	192
Lemon Meringue Tart, Green's	packet			1156
Lemon Pudding, Green's				
made up	packet			1155
Luxury Yoghurt Cheesecake, Green's	packet			1076
Macaroni Pudding, Co-op	tinned	425	15	380
Mandarin & Lemon Whip, Eden Vale	carton			125
Mandarin Royale, cold dessert, St Michael	carton			145
Meringue, average		28	1	110
Mince Pie: average		28	1	111
Mr Kipling	each			204

		g	oz	Cal.
Mixed fruit pudding, average		28	1	92
Mixed Fruit Sponge, Heinz	tin	300	10½	920
Olde English Fruit Pie, Mr Kipling	each			150
Parfait, all flavours, Chambourcy	carton			140
Peach Dessert Mix, Boots	sachet			65
Peach Melba, Birds Eye	carton			128
Peach Trifle, St Ivel	carton			165
Pineapple Papaya Delight, Tree Free	packet	100	3½	374
Pineapple in Passion Juice with Kirsch, Sainsbury	packet	283	10	172
Profiterole Mix, Mary Baker Nabisco Frear	packet			935
Queen of puddings, average		28	1	129
Raspberry Bakewell Tart, Mr Kipling	each			1280
Raspberry Cheesecake, Eden Vale	carton			200
Raspberry Fruit Sundae, Chambourcy	carton			120
Raspberry & Redcurrant Tart, Sainsbury, small	each			275

		g	oz	Cal.
Raspberry Jam Sponge Pudding, Heinz		300	10½	850
Raspberry Trifle, Eden Vale	carton			156
Rhubarb Tart, Sainsbury, small	each			270
Rice Creamola, Sun-pat		225	9	910
Rice Pudding, Co-op	tinned	170	6	155
Rum Baba, McVitie's	each			205
Sago Pudding, Co-op	tinned	425	15	350
Semolina Pudding, Co-op	tinned	425	15	365
Spicy Apple & Sultana Pudding Tiffany's	each			1380
Strawberry Dalky Supreme, Chambourcy	carton			120
Strawberry Fool, Tesco	packet			138
Strawberry Fruit Fruitfull, Beddington's	packet	142	5	180
Strawberry Jam Sponge Pudding, Heinz	tinned	300	10½	855
Strawberry Mousse, Sainsbury	carton			175
Strawberry Sundae Special, Chambourcy	each			120
Strawberry Tarts, McVitie's	packet			115
Strawberry Whip, St Michael	carton			95

		g	oz	Cal.
Tangy Lemon Cheesecake:				
Chambourcy	tub			250
Granny Smith Mix	packet			1520
Traditional Rice Pudding,				
Ambrosia		439	15½	472
Treacle Sponge Pudding, Heinz	tinned	300	10½	865
Treacle Tart, Mr Kipling		28	1	100
Trifle Mix, Bird's, made up	packet			1280
Tropical Fruit Sundae,				
Chambourcy	carton			105
Viola Topping, Chambourcy				
Supreme Dessert		28	1	41

FROZEN PUDDINGS AND ICE CREAM

		g	oz	Cal.
Apple Dessert, McVitie's cake	each			490
Apple Cream Slice, McVitie's				
cake	each			240
Apple Pie, McVitie's	each			1600
Apricot Padua, Bertorelli		28	1	50
Arctic Circle, Birds Eye	each			155
Arctic Gâteau, Birds Eye	each			500

		g	oz	Cal.
Arctic Log, Birds Eye	each			600
Arctic Roll, Birds Eye	each			450
Baked Lemon Cheesecake, St Michael	carton			475
Big Dipper, Wall's: strawberry	each			110
vanilla	each			110
Big Feast, Wall's	each			232
Black Cherry Ice Cream, Continental Dairy, Waitrose		28	1	53
Black Cherry Ripple, Lyons Maid cutting brick	each			909
Blackcurrant Cheesecake, McVitie's	each			1360
Bubble Ball, Lyons Maid	each			102
Caramel Toffee Ice Cream, Waitrose		28	1	57
Cheesecake:				
Apple & Blackberry, Ross		28	1	65
Blackcurrant, Sainsbury	packet			1300
Strawberry Birds Eye	each			1560
Chipwich, Lyons Maid Individual Ice Cream	each			343
Chocolate Almond Ice Cream, Lyons Maid Gold Seal 100ml (3½ fl oz)				139

	g	oz	Cal.
Chocolate Chip American Style Ice Cream, St Michael	28	1	75
Chocolate Gâteau, Birds Eye	each		1200
Chocolate Ice Cream, St Michael	28	1	7
Chocolate Mint Ice Cream, Lyons Maid	each		168
Chocolate Ripple Ice Cream, Lyons Maid	brick		925
Chocolate Soft-Scoop Ice Cream, Safeway	28	1	51
Chocolate Swirl Ice Cream, Lyons Maid Gold Seal	28	1	54
Choux Buns, Birds Eye	each		120
Cider Quench Ice Cream, Lyons Maid	each		34
Coconut Flake Ice Cream, Lyons Maid	each		172
Coffee Mandarin Gâteau, Ross	28	1	85
Cola Quench Ice Cream, Lyons Maid	each		38
Cornetto, Chocolate & Nut, Wall's	each		195
Cornetto, Rum & Raisin, Wall's	each		195

	g	oz	Cal.
Cornish Dairy Ice Cream, Lyons Maid	brick		903
Cornish Raspberry Sundae, Lyons Maid	each		97
Cornish Vanilla Chocolate Ice Cream, Lyons Maid	each		126
Dairy Black Cherry Gâteau, Bertorelli	piece		205
Dairy Black Cherry Ice Cream, Lyons Maid (Napoli)	50	2	100
Dairy Choc Menthe Ice Cream, Bertorelli	50	2	130
Dairy Choc 'n' Nut Cone, Bejam	each		275
Dairy Chocolate Ice Cream, Bertorelli	50	2	120
Dairy Coffee Ice Cream, Bertorelli	50	2	110
Dairy Cornish Ice Cream, Ross Tudor	50	2	90
Dairy Cream Sponge, Findus	50	2	200
Dairy ice cream, average	50	2	130
Dairy Mela Menthe Ice Cream, Bertorelli	each		120

	g	oz	Cal.
Dairy Mela Parisienne Ice Cream, Bertorelli	each		210
Dairy Mela Stregata Ice Cream, Bertorelli	each		210
Dairy Nutty Toffee Ice Cream, Lyons Maid (Napoli)	50	2	110
Dairy Peach Melba Ice Cream, Lyons Maid (Napoli)	50	2	90
Dairy Praline Ice Cream, Bertorelli	50	2	120
Dairy Strawberry Ice Cream, Bertorelli	50	2	100
Dairy Strawberry Ice Cream, Lyons Maid (Napoli)	50	2	90
Dairy Tutti Fruitti Ice Cream, Lyons Maid (Napoli)	50	2	100
Dairy Vanilla Ice Cream, Bertorelli	50	2	115
Dairy Vanilla Ice Cream, Lyons Maid (Napoli)	50	2	100
Dark & Golden Choc Bar, Wall's	each		130
Dark Satin Choc Ice, Lyons Maid	each		130
Double Choc Bar, Wall's	each		160

	g	oz	Cal.
Dracula Ice Lolly, Wall's each			50
Eclair, Birds Eye each			126
Fruit & Nut Sundae, Wimpy portion			235
Golden Orange Ice Cream, Lyons Maid each			55
Golden Vanilla Choc Bar, Wall's each			130
Golden Vanilla Ice Cream Bar, Wall's each			85
Gold Seal Choc Nut Sundae, Lyons Maid each			95
Gold Seal Raspberry Sundae, Lyons Maid each			75
Hazelnut Siena Ice Cream, Bertorelli	50	2	135
Ice cream: average	28	1	45
Mr Whippy's	28	1	46
Ice cream Bar:			
Wall's Cornish each			90
Wall's Golden Vanilla each			85
Ice Cream Float, Wimpy portion			190
Ice Cream Mix, Pearce Duff packet			320
Ice Cream Pancakes, Daloon each			110
Ice Cream Roll, Co-op each			340

	g	oz	Cal.
Ice Cream Sundae, Wimpy	portion		240
Italiano, Wall's Chocolate & Nut Capri	each		115
Italiano, Wall's Tutti Frutti Classico	each		107
Juice Bar, Lyons Maid	each		45
K9, Wall's	each		50
King Cone, Lyons Maid:			
Chocolate	each		220
Cornish Dairy	each		210
Strawberry	each		190
Knickerbocker Glory, Wimpy	portion		240
Lemon Cream Pie, Findus	28	1	103
Lemon Cream Torte, Sainsbury	packet		1980
Lemon Curd Sherbert Ice Cream, Baskin Robbins	28	1	46
Lemon Surprise, Bertorelli	each		150
Lemon Torte, Ross	28	1	71
Light Choc Ice, Frederick's	each		125
Maple Walnut Ice Cream, Hortons	28	1	57
Melon Ravenna Water Ice, Bertorelli	28	1	57

	g	oz	Cal.
Midnight Mini Choc Bar, Wall's	each		141
Mini Brick, Lyons Maid	each		55
Mini Choc Bar, Wall's	each		46
Mini Fruit Bar, Wall's	each		32
Mint Choc Chip, Lyons Maid			
Gold Seal 143ml (¼ pint)			151
Mint Choc Croccante, Wall's			
Italiano range	50	2	122
Mint Choc Ices, Frederick's	each		125
Mint Chocolate Supreme			
Dessert, Chambourcy	28	1	35
Mini Waffles, Birds Eye	each		20
Mint Neapolitan, Lyons Maid			
Soft Scoop	28	1	52
Mr Men, Lyons Maid Ice Cream	each		27
Mousse, Ross	carton		104
Neapolitan Ice Cream:			
Lyons Maid cutting brick	each		830
Lyons Maid family brick	each		400
non-dairy, St Michael	28	1	50
Ross	28	1	51
soft-scoop: Bejam	28	1	50
Waitrose	28	1	52
New York Butter Almond			
Ice Cream, Wall's	28	1	63

	g	oz	Cal.
Nut Meringue Gâteau, McVitie's	each		1405
Orange Fruitie Ice Lolly, Wall's	each		60
Orange Maid Ice Cream, Lyons Maid	each		49
Orange Maid, Lyons Maid	each		50
Orange Surprise, Bertorelli	portion		175
Passion Fruit Cocktail Cup Italiano, Wall's	each		105
Peach Melba Ice Cream, Lyons Maid	brick		920
Peach Melba Soft Scoop Bulk Ice Cream, Lyons Maid	28	1	50
Pineapple Juice Bar, Lyons Maid	each		46
Pineapple Split, Wall's	each		90
Plum Pudding & Rum Sauce, Ross	each		300
Pola Maid, Lyons Maid	each		50
Profiterole Choux, Ross	28	1	114
Raspberry Dessert Flan, Lyons Maid	28	1	75
Raspberry Ripple: Tesco	28	1	32
Ripple	brick		312
Raspberry Romano, Wall's	28	1	46

	g	oz	Cal.
Raspberry Royale, St Michael	carton			140
Raspberry Supermousse, Birds Eye	carton			120
Raspberry Tart, McVitie's	each			125
Raspberry/Vanilla Double Mousse, Findus	tub			90
Raspberry Water Ice, Lyons Maid		28	1	22
Raspberry and Redcurrant Cheesecake, St Michael		28	1	81
Real Milk Ice, Lyons Maid	each			50
Rhum Baba, Ross	each			340
Rich Chocolate Ripple, Lyons Maid		28	1	50
Roast Almond Chocolate, Lyons Maid		100	3½	545
Rock Around the Choc, Lyons Maid	each			130
Rocket Ice Cream, Lyons Maid	each			30
Rocky Road, Baskin Robbins Single Scoop Ice Cream	each			185
Skull, Lyons Maid	each			80
Strawberry & Vanilla Family Brick, Ross Tudor		50	2	110

	g	oz	Cal.
Strawberry Cheesecake, BhS each			260
Strawberry Cream Cake, McVitie's each			1015
Strawberry Cream Flan, McVitie's each			855
Strawberry Cup Italiano, Wall's each			125
Strawberry Gâteau, Birds Eye each			1680
Strawberry Ice Cream, Bejam Soft Scoop	50	2	95
Strawberry Ice Cream, Walls's Cornish Dairy, Soft Scoop	50	2	100
Strawberry Marshmallow Sundae, Wall's brick			560
Strawberry Mivvi, Lyons Maid each			80
Strawberry Party Gâteau, McVitie's each			1400
Strawberry Split, Wall's each			80
Strawberry Sundae, Wimpy each			140
Strawberry Twin Ice Cream, Lyons Maid Soft Scoop	50	2	105
Supermousse, Birds Eye:			
Mint Choc Chip carton			140
Raspberry carton			118
Syllabub, Eden Vale carton			185

		g	oz	Cal.
Swiss Mountain Strawberry Ice Cream, Wall's		50	2	105
Toffee Crumble Ice Cream, Lyons Maid	each			180
Toffee Crunch Sundae, Wall's, family size	each			590
Toffee Fudge Caramella, Wall's Italiano range		28	1	55
Toffee Ripple, Lyons Maid, family brick	each			430
Tom & Jerry Lolly, Wall's	each			50
Traditional Vanilla Ice Cream, Bejam Soft Scoop		28	1	44
Twin Lolly, Lyons Maid	each			35
Value Ice Cream Roll, Bejam	each			330
Vanilla Bar, Lyons Maid	each			70
Vanilla Choc Flake, Lyons Maid Gold Seal 143ml (¼ pint)				172
Vanilla Ice Cream:				
Baskin Robbins		70	2½	142
Bejam Soft Scoop		28	1	44
Horton's		28	1	49
Tesco Easy Scoop		28	1	46
Vanilla Kup, Lyons Maid	each			86

	g	oz	Cal.
Vanilla & Strawberry Ripple, Co-op	28	1	33
Viennetta, Wall's Special	each		816
Waffles: Findus	28	1	87
St Michael	28	1	38
Water ice, average	28	1	20
West Country Cream Vanilla Ice, Wall's	28	1	51
Woppa, Wall's	each		40
Zoom, Lyons Maid	each		44

RICE AND RICE DISHES

Boil-in-the-Bag Rice, Kellogg's		28	1	94
Chicken Curry, Batchelor's Vesta Meal	portion		411
Chicken Savoury Rice, Batchelor's	packet		430
Golden Rice, Batchelor's	packet		440
Mild Curry, Batchelor's Savoury Rice	packet		465
Paella: Birds Eye	as sold		270
Vesta	each helping		330
Pilau Rice, Olaf Foods	packet		234

		g	oz	Cal.
Pot Rice, Chicken Risotto, Golden Wonder	packet			215
Rice, brown: boiled		28	1	30
raw		28	1	100
white: boiled		28	1	35
raw		28	1	102
Rice, Peas & Mushrooms, Birds Eye	packet	227	8	318
Risotto, KP	tub			150
Sweet & Sour Savoury Rice, Batchelor's	packet			660
Tomato Savoury Rice, Safeway	packet			470
Tropical Fruit Savoury Rice, Batchelor's	packet			435
Yang Chow Fried Rice	pack	170	6	305

SALADS

		g	oz	Cal.
American Bean, Green Giant		482	17	345
American Super, Crosse & Blackwell	tin			250
Apple, peach & nut, average		28	1	58
Celery, Apple & Orange, Mattessons		28	1	55

	g	oz	Cal.
Chicken & Sweetcorn, Eden Vale	28	1	44
Coleslaw, Chambourcy	100	3½	150
Country, Eden Vale	28	1	35
Crispy, in Vinaigrette, St Ivel	28	1	20
Dill & Chives Salad Days, Knorr	packet		15
Egg & Cheese Potato with salad filling, Spud-U-Like	each		550
Florida, St Michael	227	8	465
French in Vinaigrette:			
Mattessons	227	8	185
Sainsbury	227	8	185
Ham Salad, Mattessons	28	1	60
Malaysian, Crosse & Blackwell	tin		180
Maryland, Eden Vale	160	5½	252
Picnic, BhS	226	8	290
Potato: Eden Vale	28	1	41
Heinz	tinned	210	17½	400
St Michael	227	8	730
Potato & Chive: Eden Vale	227	8	330
Sainsbury	28	1	480
Potato & Smoked Bacon, BhS	150	5½	435
Prawn, average	142	5	150

		g	oz	Cal.
Prawn coleslaw, average		200	7	215
Spanish: Eden Vale		28	1	30
Sainsbury		170	6	355
Spicy with Mixed Peppers, Eden Vale		170	6	240
Spring, Mattessons		170	6	300
Tropical Fruit & Pasta, Eden Vale		170	6	222
Tuna, BhS		150	5½	455
Vegetable: Co-op	carton	142	5	210
Eden Vale	carton	227	8	320
Mattessons		170	6	205
Waldorf, St Ivel		28	1	38

SAUCES, STUFFINGS AND DRESSINGS

SAVOURY

		g	oz	Cal.
Au Poivre Sauce, Crosse & Blackwell	sachet			355
Barbecue Dry Sauce Mix, Colman's		28	1	88

	g	oz	Cal.
Beef Bourguignon, Colman's Cooking Mix	28	1	99
Beef Carbonade, Cook-in-the-Pot, Crosse & Blackwell	28	1	115
Beef Goulash, Cook-in-the-Pot, Crosse & Blackwell	28	1	108
Beef Provençale, Colman's Casserole Mix	28	1	79
Beef Stroganoff, Cook-in-the-Pot, Crosse & Blackwell	28	1	119
Blue Cheese Dressing:			
Sainsbury	tablespoon		80
Kraft	28	1	137
Bolognese Sauce:			
Buitoni	tin		144
Campbells Prego Sauce	28	1	28
Bread Sauce:			
fresh, average	1 tablespoon		15
Colman's Dry Mix	28	1	89
Brown Ale Sauce, HP Country Cooking Sauce	28	1	13
Brown Sauce, Gateway	28	1	30
Burgundy Wine Sauce, Baxter's Cooking-in-Sauce	28	1	59

	g	oz	Cal.
Chicken Chasseur, Cook-in-the-Pot, Crosse & Blackwell	28	1	110
Chicken Seasoning, Colman's Dry Sauce Mix	28	1	102
Classic French Salad Dressing, Kraft	28	1	45
Cooking-in-Sauce, Baxter's:			
Burgundy	28	1	59
Medium Curry	28	1	87
Sauce Provençale	28	1	113
Sweet 'n' Sour	28	1	107
White Wine	28	1	111
Country Cooking Sauce, HP:			
cider	28	1	13
tomato & herb	28	1	9
Creamy Cucumber Salad Dressing, Kraft	28	1	144
Curry dressing, average	28	1	42
Curry Sauce, Homepride	pack		555
Daddies Favourite, HP	28	1	15
Daddies Tomato Ketchup, HP	28	1	30
Daddies Tomato Sauce, HP	28	1	20
Dansak Classic Curry Sauce, Homepride	383	13½	440

	g	oz	Cal.
Egg mayonnaise, average helping			260
English Herb Dressing, Alfonal	28	1	100
French dressing: average 1 tablespoon			75
oil free 1 tablespoon			3
Garlic & Herb Stuffing Mix, Knorr packet			370
Garlic Salad Dressing, St Michael	28	1	185
Gravy:			
Lite, McCormicks Gravy Mix, made up 3 tablespoons			9
powder, Bisto 2 tablespoons			4
thick, average, made with dripping 2 tablespoons			30
Hazelnut & Herb Stuffing Mix:			
average	28	1	121
Knorr packet			383
Hot Taco Sauce, Old El Paso	28	1	10
HP Fruity Sauce	28	1	24
HP Mint Sauce	28	1	25
HP Sauce	28	1	21
Ideal Sauce, Heinz	28	1	35
Irish White Salad Dressing, St Michael	28	1	115

		g	oz	Cal.
Italian Garlic Dressing, Kraft		28	1	125
Korma Authentic Curry Sauce, Sharwood	tin	283	10	405
Korma Classic Curry Sauce, Homepride	tin	380	13½	380
Korma Curry Mix, Colman's	packet			145
Lamb Ragout, Cook-in-the-Pot, Crosse & Blackwell		28	1	118
Lemon & Parsley Sauce, Homepride	packet			150
Madeira Wine Gravy, Crosse & Blackwell	sachet			383
Madras Curry: Olaf Foods	packet			281
Oxo	packet			310
Madras Curry Sauce, Homepride	tinned	383	13½	380
Mayonnaise: average		28	1	205
Burgess		28	1	172
Hellmann's		28	1	100
Milanese Sauce, Buitoni	tinned	283	10	120
Mild Taco Sauce, Old El Paso		28	1	10
Mint Jelly:				
Colman's bottled sauce		28	1	26
Frank Cooper		28	1	78

		g	oz	Cal.
Mint sauce, average	1 teaspoon			5
Mornay Master Sauce, Colman's	packet			148
Mushroom Gravy Mix, McCormick		28	1	9
Mushroom Ketchup, Burgess		28	1	6
Mushroom Sauce Mix, Colman's	packet			95
Napolitan Sauce: Buitoni	tin			76
Campbells	tinned	28	1	26
Navarin of Lamb, Colman's Casserole Mix		28	1	92
OK Fruity Sauce, Colman's		28	1	26
Onion Dressing with Chives, St Michael		28	1	106
Onion Dry Sauce Mix, Colman's		28	1	67
Onion & Parsley Sauce, Knorr Salad Days	sachet			20
Onion & Pepper Sauce for Spaghetti, Buitoni	tin			120
Onion sauce, average		28	1	25
Onion Sauce Mix: Colman's	packet			80
Safeway	sachet			110
Parsley & Chives Salad Dressing, Knorr	sachet			20

	g	oz	Cal.
Parsley Sauce: Colman's Mix packet			100
Knorr Mix packet			73
Parsley & Thyme Stuffing:			
Paxo mix packet			292
Whitworth's mix packet	85	3	300
Paysan Bonne Cuisine Sauce,			
Crosse & Blackwell packet			105
Pork, Colman's Casserole Mix	28	1	84
Prawn Cocktail Sauce, Burgess	28	1	80
Private Label Salad Cream, HP	28	1	89
Red Wine Sauce, Knorr tin	28	1	101
Rogan Josh Curry Sauce,			
Homepride tinned	383	13½	383
Sage & Onion Stuffing: Knorr packet			355
Paxo packet			300
Salad Cream, Crosse &			
Blackwell 1 tablespoon			50
Sauce Provençale, Baxter's			
Cooking-in-Sauce tin			400
Sauce Tartare, Burgess	28	1	75
Seafood Dressing, Pearce &			
Duff	28	1	135
Seafood Sauce, Knorr mix packet			175

		g	oz	Cal.
Soured Cream & Chives, Hellmann's	tub			85
Sunflower Dressing, Flora	1 tablespoon			75
Tandoori Marinade Curry Mix, Colman's	packet			92
Tartare Sauce: average		28	1	82
Frank Cooper		28	1	88
Pearce Duff		28	1	82
Sharwood		28	1	80
Thousand Island Dressing:				
Hellmann's		28	1	155
Kraft		28	1	121
St Michael		28	1	160
Tomato, Bacon & Ham Omelette Mate, Campbells	tin	142	5	150
Tomato Ketchup:				
average		28	1	28
Crosse & Blackwell		28	1	29
Tomato & Onion Cook-in-Sauce, Homepride	tin	376	13½	260
Tomato Sauce, Sainsbury		28	1	35
Vinaigrette, Eden Vale		28	1	9
Vindaloo Authentic Curry Sauce, Sharwood	tinned	283	10	390

		g	oz	Cal.
Vindaloo, Homepride Classic Curry Sauce	tinned	383	13½	490
Vinegar & Oil Dressing, Tesco		28	1	43
Walnut Dressing, St Michael	28ml/1 fl oz			118
White sauce, savoury, average		28	1	41
White Wine Sauce:				
Baxter's Cook-in-Sauce	tinned	28	1	111
Crosse & Blackwell	tinned	283	10	143
Worcestershire Sauce, Lea & Perrins		29	1	20
Yogurt & Chive Dressing, Heinz		28	1	82
Yoghurt & Cucumber Dressing, Hellmann's		28	1	163

SAUCES, STUFFINGS AND DRESSINGS

SWEET

	g	oz	Cal.
Bramley Apple Sauce, Pan-Yan	28	1	16
Brandy butter, average	28	1	170
Butterscotch Sauce, Lyons Maid	28	1	90
Caramel Topping, Colman's	28	1	85

		g	oz	Cal.
Cranberry Jelly:				
average		28	1	40
jellied, Baxter's		28	1	71
Desserts Sauces, all flavours, Wall's		28	1	80
Dream Topping, Bird's	packet			355
Golden syrup, average	1 tablespoon			60
Maple syrup, average		28	1	68
Profiteroles Sauce, frozen, Ross		28	1	96
Redcurrant Sauce, John West	tinned	99	3½	210
Strawberry Dessert Sauce, HP		28	1	50
Treacle, black, average		28	1	72
Whip Topping, Rich's	30ml/1 fl oz			20
White Sauce, Sweet		28	1	47

SAVOURY SNACKS AND CRISPS

		g	oz	Cal.
Alien Spacers, KP	packet	26	¾	120
Bacon Bites, Tesco	packet			230
Bacon Crispies, Sainsbury	packet	50	1¾	235
Bacon Crisps, KP	packet			150

		g	oz	Cal.
Bacon Puffs, Tesco	packet	50	1¾	245
Bacon Streaks, Safeway	packet	50	1¾	230
Barbecue Spare Rib Crisps, St Michael		28	1	138
Bones Crisps, Smiths	packet			95
Brontosaurus Ribs, Sainsbury	packet	25	1	118
Butterkist Popcorn		28	1	111
Cheese & Celery Sticks Biscuit, Huntley & Palmer	each			22
Cheeselets, Peek Frean	each			3
Cheese & Ham Bites, Tesco	packet	75	2½	375
Cheese & Onion Puffs, Tesco	packet	50	2	255
Cheese Puffs, Gateway		28	1	145
Cheese Sandwich Biscuits, Waitrose	each			45
Cheese Thins, Gateway		28	1	152
Cheesy Corn Curls, Gateway		28	1	128
Cheese & Onion Flavour Savouries Biscuit, Limmits Meal Replacement	each meal			250
Cheese Flavour Cracker Biscuit with Bran, Limmits Meal Replacement Biscuit	each meal			248

		g	oz	Cal.
Crinkles, St Michael	packet	100	3½	530
Crunch 'n' Slim Biscuit, Crunch 'n' Slim (2 biscuits)	each meal			234
Disco: all flavours, KP	packet			145
ready salted, KP	packet			150
Frazzles, Smiths	smallest packet	26	1	120
Good 'n' Crunchy Crisps, Salt & Vinegar, KP		35	1¼	190
Hula Hoops, KP:				
salt & barbecue	packet	28	1	165
salt & vinegar	packet	28	1	160
Lamb Savouries, Brooks	each			205
Loops, savoury snack, St Michael		28	1	136
Minced Beef Savoury Toast, warmed, Findus	each			140
Monster Munch, Smiths	packet	26	1	134
Mumbo Jumbos, all flavours, Holly Mills	packet	20	¾	87
Natural Wheel Savoury Snacks, BhS		43		214
Peanut Butter Wheateats, Allinson	each			60

		g	oz	Cal.
Peanut & Sesame Cookies, Holly Mills	each			54
Piccolos, savoury snack, Sainsbury	packet	50	2	250
Pizza Cracker Biscuit, Sainsbury	each			10
Popcorn, average		28	1	137
Pork scratchings, average		28	1	185
Potato Rings: St Michael	packet	75	2½	385
Sainsbury	packet	28	1	130
Tesco	packet	75	2½	390
Potato Sticks, Waitrose	packet	113	4	575
Potato Swirls, Sainsbury		50	1¾	210
Potato Thins, St Michael		50	1¾	255
Prawn Cocktail Snacks, Tesco		50	2	255
Prawn Cocktail Wickers, KP		23	¾	100
Prawn Shells, BhS		43	1½	210
Quavers, Smiths	packet	18	½	93
Ready Salted Crisps: BhS	packet	25	1	142
KP	packet	25	1	155
Ringos, all flavours, Golden Wonder	packet	21	¾	97
Salt & Vinegar Chips, BhS	packet			215
Salt & Vinegar Crisps, BhS	packet	64	2¼	340

		g	oz	Cal.
Samosa Roll, Chic-o-Roll	each			165
Savoury Hungarian Snacks, Prewetts	pack	50	1¾	160
Savoury Puffs, Safeway	packet			300
Savoury Twigs, Safeway	packet	50	1¾	200
Scampi Fries, Smiths	smallest packet			115
Sesame Cracker, Waitrose	each			20
Skips, KP		16	½	80
Skydivers, KP		18	½	80
Snaps, Walkers	packet	14	½	75
Snax, Sainsbury	each			15
Square Crisps, Smiths	smallest packet	25	1	135
Toasty Grills, Danish Prime	each			300
Tubes, Smiths:				
Cheese & Onion	packet			120
Salt & Vinegar	packet			115
Tuc, Savoury Sandwich Biscuit, McVitie's	each			73
Turkey Savouries, Tiffany's		92	3¾	175
Twiglets: Peak Frean	long, each			5
Sainsbury	short, each			3
Twists, Smiths	packet			85

		g	oz	Cal.
Wholemeal Toasties, Granose	packet	200	7½	300
Wotsits, Cheesy, Golden Wonder	packet	23	¾	135
Worcester Sauce Crisps, KP		25	¾	148

SIMPLY FOR SLIMMERS

		g	oz	Cal.
Apricots, in low calorie syrup, Boots	tinned	220	7¾	35
Beeflike Flavour, Soyapro Protein Food		28	1	59
Beef Risotto, Batchelor's Slim-a-Meal	packet			245
Boldo Tablet, Potter's Herbal Supplies	each			18
Cambridge Diet Meal Bar, Chocolate Flavour	bar	52	1¾	140
Cambridge Diet Meal, Chicken Flavour Soup Mix	sachet	34	1¾	110
Canderel, sweetener	tablet			9
Cheese & Onion Flavour Savouries, Limmits Meal Replacement Biscuit	meal			250

	g	oz	Cal.
Cheese Flavour Cracker Biscuit with Bran, Limmits Meal Replacement Biscuit	meal		248
Chocolate Digestive Biscuit Meal, Limmits Meal Replacement Biscuit	meal		306
Crunch 'n' Slim Biscuit, Crunch 'n' Slim (2 biscuits)	meal		234
Dietdays, Healthcrafts Meal Replacement Biscuit	28	1	125
Fibretrim, Healthcrafts Meal Replacement Biscuit	28	1	14
Figure Trim, Health & Diet Food Co	capsule		8
Five Day Place Replacement, Healthcrafts	28	1	101
Formula 3+6, Health & Diet Food Co	capsule		8
Fortify Meal Replacement	sachet	44	1½	200
Fruit Cocktail in low calorie syrup, Boots		220	7¾	50
Fruit & Nut, Meal Replacement Chocolate Bar, Boots	each		340
Glucose, liquid, BP		28	1	90
Granulated Sweetener, Sugaree		28	1	102

	g	oz	Cal.
Hazelnut Meal Replacement Bar, Boots	each		335
Lessen, Slimmers' Product	meal		148
Low Calorie Coleslaw, Eden Vale	160	5½	115
Low Calorie Dressing, Heidelberg	28	1	16
Low Calorie French Mayonnaise, Sainsbury	28	1	85
Low Calorie Salad Dressing, Burgess	28	1	35
Low Calorie Tomato Ketchup, Weight Watchers	28	1	15
Low Calorie Vinaigrette, Kraft	28	1	30
Low fat spread, average	28	1	5
Low Fat Natural 1, Speise Quark Soft Cheese, Nordmilch	28	1	158
Low Fat Soft Cheese, Safeway	28	1	26
Low Fat Soft Cheese with Apricots, Senoble	28	1	40
Low Fat Spread:			
Outline	28	1	105
Weight Watchers	28	1	100
Low Sugar Jam, Energen	28	1	36

		g	oz	Cal.
Mayonnaise, Weight Watchers		28	1	86
Meal Replacement Drink, Boots	each			140
Milk Chocolate Sweetmeal with Bran, Limmits Meal Replacement Biscuit	meal			248
Minced Soya & Onion Mix, Direct Foods		28	1	100
Muesli: with Bran, Limmits	meal			252
sugar free, Sunpure		28	1	96
Sugarfree, Holly Mills		28	1	102
Muesli Meal Replacement Bar, Boots	each			195
Natural Protoveg, Direct Foods		28	1	80
Nut & Raisin Carob Bar, no sugar, Kalibu	each	42	1½	208
Oil, Limmits Spray & Fry		28	1	220
Orange Flavour with Bran, Limmits Replacement Meal Biscuit	meal			250
Orange Marmalade, Country Basket, sugar-free jam		28	1	35
Outline Low Fat Spread		28	1	105
Oxtail Soup:				
Co-op	tinned	425	15	180
Waistline, low calorie		283	10	65
Heinz, low calorie		295	10½	75

		g	oz	Cal.
Peaches in low calorie syrup, Boots		200	7½	46
Pineapple, in low calorie syrup, Boots	tinned	220	7¾	55
Pineapple Dance Complete Shaping Slim Plan, Weider	each			200
Plain Meal Replacement Chocolate Bar, Boots	each			308
Protose, Granose	tinned	248	10	455
Prune Yogurt, Waistline		125	4½	71
Shape Milk, St Ivel	568ml/1 pint			255
Shapers Low Calorie Dressing, Boots	1 tablespoon			25
Slender Bar, Carnation Meal Replacement	each			126
Slender Crunch Bar, Carnation Meal Replacement	each			126
Slender Yoghurt Enriched, Carnation Replacement Meal	sachet			108
Slim Bran Biscuit, Blakey's	each			35
Slim Choc, Carnation	sachet			38
Slimgard Brunch, Slimgard	meal			141
Slimgard Crunch Bar, Slimgard	each			145

	g	oz	Cal.
Slimgard Liquid Meal Replacement, strawberry, Slimgard	meal		325
Slim Soup, Carnation	sachet		40
Slimway Low Calorie Salad Dressing, Heinz	1 tablespoon		25
Slimmer's sugar, Sucron	28	1	108
Slymbar, Holly Mills	each		115
Slymbred, Blakey's: brown	slice		10
white	slice		10
Slymsnack, Blakey's	each		90
Slymsquare Biscuit, Blakey's	each		30
Soup:			
Golden Vegetable, Crosse & Blackwell low calorie	283	10	50
Spring Vegetable, Heinz low calorie	tin	295	10½	65
Tomato: Boots Shaper Soup	tin	290	10¼	56
Heinz low calorie	tin	295	10½	75
Knorr, low calorie	packet		40
Turkey Broth, Boots Shaper Soup	tin	290	10¼	47
Vegetable: Boots Shaper Soup	tin	290	10¼	56
Heinz low calorie	tin	295	10½	70

		g	oz	Cal.
Sprinkle Sweet, Hermesetas		28	1	100
Strawberry Yogurt, Waistline	carton	125	4½	75
Sugar Free Drinking Chocolate, Carnation				
made up with skimmed milk	packet			330
made up with whole milk	packet			435
Sweet 'n' Slim, Slimcea		28	1	108
Sweetener, Sweetex Powder		28	1	100
Vanilla Flavour with Bran, Limmits Replacement Biscuit	meal			250
Vita Fiber, Bayer Tablet		28	1	51
Waistline Oil-free French Dressing, Crosse & Blackwell		28	1	5
Waistline Seafood Sauce, Crosse & Blackwell		28	1	42
Waistline Tartare Sauce, Crosse & Blackwell		28	1	43
Waistline Tomato Ketchup, Crosse & Blackwell		28	1	17
Weight Watchers Ice Cream Brick, Lyons Maid	brick			527
Weiners, Granose	tin	385	13½	811
Whole Earth No Sugar Ketchup, Harmony		28	1	36

		g	oz	Cal.
Yogurt:				
diet, strawberry, Ski		125	4½	50
low fat, rhubarb, Sainsbury		125	4½	54

SOUPS

		g	oz	Cal.
Asparagus: Campbells Superior		295	10½	180
Knorr Quick	sachet			48
Barbecue Beef & Tomato, Batchelor's		28	1	48
Beef Broth, Baxter's		28	1	13
Boston Bean, Knorr	packet	28	1	270
Chicken & Leek, Batchelor's Cup-a-Soup		28	1	26
Chicken & Mushroom, Batchelor's 5 Minute Soup		28	1	62
Chicken Noodle, Knorr	packet			187
Chicken & Vegetable Broth with Rice, Campbells Granny		28	1	10
Cock-a-Leekie, Baxter's		28	1	60
Crab Bisque, Campbells		28	1	21
Cream of Asparagus, Baxter's	tinned	425	15	264
Cream of Celery, Heinz		28	1	264

		g	oz	Cal.
Cream of Chicken, Campbells Condensed	tin			28
Cream of Mushroom, Crosse & Blackwell		28	1	15
Cream of Pheasant, Baxter's	tin			235
Cream of Scampi, Baxter's	tin			275
Crofters Thick Vegetable, Knorr	packet			250
Game Consommé, Baxter's	tin	425	15	50
Golden Chicken & Mushroom, Heinz	tinned	300	10½	155
Golden Pea with Ham, Campbells Granny Soup		425	15	250
Golden Vegetable: Batchelor's	550ml/1 pint/ packet			215
Batchelor's Cup-a-Soup	packet			70
Harvest Vegetable & Beef, Crosse & Blackwell Pot Soup	sachet			75
Harvest Vegetable & Chicken, Batchelor's		28	1	62
Ham, Turkey & Vegetable, Campbells Main Course		28	1	17
Highlander's Broth, Baxter's	tin			147

		g	oz	Cal.
Highland Lentil, Knorr	packet			301
Highland Scotch Broth, Knorr	packet			257
Italian Tomato & Vegetable, Batchelor's made up packet	575 ml/1 pint			150
Lentil: Campbells	tin	142	5	125
Co-op	tin	425	15	420
Lobster Bisque: Baxter's		425	15	180
Crosse & Blackwell Speciality Soup	tin	425	15	95
Lobster, Sainsbury	tin	425	15	187
Macaroni Beef, Campbells Granny Soup	tinned	425	15	434
Maryland with Sweetcorn, Knorr	575 ml/1 pint			265
Minestrone: Batchelor's Cup-a-Soup with Croutons	575ml/1 pint packet			70
Knorr	575ml/1 pint packet			174
Sainsbury	575ml/1 pint packet			125
Mulligatawny, Heinz	tinned	435	15¼	256
Mushroom Cup-a-Soup, Batchelor's	sachet			116

		g	oz	Cal.
Mushroom, Safeway	packet			118
Onion, Cup-a-Soup, Batcehlor's	sachet			110
Oxtail:				
Batchelor's, made up	575ml/1 pint			160
Baxter's	tinned	425	15	185
Campbells Bumper Harvest	tin	425	15	185
Crosse & Blackwell	575ml/1 pint			170
Heinz	tin	300	10½	145
Safeway	tin			130
Sainsbury	575ml/1 pint			
	packet			120
Supermug	tub			85
Tesco		425	15	230
Pea & Ham:				
Baxter's	tinned	425	15	225
Campbells Main Course	tinned	425	15	360
Crosse & Blackwell Box Soup	575ml/1 pint			173
Heinz	tinned	300	10½	200
Knorr Mix	275ml/½ pint			70
Pheasant Consommé, Baxter's	tin			49
Poacher's Broth, Baxter's	tin			177
Rich Country Mushroom, Batchelor's	575ml/1 pint			
	packet			208
Rich Tomato, Crosse & Blackwell	sachet			80
Royal Game, Baxter's	tinned	425	15	142

SOUPS

		g	oz	Cal.
Scotch Broth, Batchelor's	575ml/1 pint			
made up	packet			135
Scottish Lentil with Vegetable, Crosse & Blackwell		283	10	125
Spring Vegetable, Crosse & Blackwell, made up	575ml/1 pint			90
Stockpot, Campbells Condensed	tin	140	5	80
Thick Chicken:				
Crosse & Blackwell	575ml/1 pint packet			174
Safeway	tin	425	15	130
Thick Country Vegetable, Crosse & Blackwell	575ml/1 pint packet			185
Thick Devon Onion, Batchelor's	575ml/1 pint packet			174
Thick Farmhouse Vegetable, Batchelor's	575ml/1pint packet			145
Thick Garden Vegetable, Crosse & Blackwell	575ml/1pint packet			140
Thick Lincoln Pea, Batchelor's	575ml/1 pint packet			245
Thick Mushroom, Batchelor's Cup-a-Soup Special	sachet			108

		g	oz	Cal.
Thick Onion, Crosse & Blackwell	575ml/1 pint packet			172
Thick Pea, Crosse & Blackwell	575ml/1 pint packet			152
Thick Savoury Vegetable, Batchelor's	575ml/1 pint			195
Tomato:				
Batchelor's Cup-a-Soup	sachet			83
Campbells Condensed	tin	140	5	90
Sainsbury	tin	283	10	162
Tomato with Prawns, Frank Cooper	tin	425	15	174
Tomato & Vegetable, Crosse & Blackwell Chunky	tin	432	15½	220
Traditional Tomato, Batchelor's	575ml/1 pint packet			262
Traditional Vegetable & Beef, Batchelor's	575ml/1 pint packet			164
Turkey, Frank Cooper	tinned	425	15	212
Turkey & Vegetable Broth, Campbells Condensed	tinned	140	5	100
Vegetable:				
Campbells Condensed	tinned	140	5	95
Tesco	tinned	425	15	155
Waitrose	tinned	28	1	14

		g	oz	Cal.
Vegetable & Beef:				
Batchelor's Cup-a-Soup	sachet			86
Crosse & Blackwell Box Soup	575ml/1 pint			152
Vichyssoise:				
Baxter's	tinned	425	15	192
Crosse & Blackwell	tinned	425	15	202
Virginia Sweetcorn, Knorr	275ml/½ pint packet			106

SPREADS AND TOPPINGS

		g	oz	Cal.
Beef Paste, Prince's	jar			161
Cucumber Spread, Heinz		28	1	62
Dairy Cheese Spread:				
Rowntree Mackintosh		28	1	75
Sun-Pat		28	1	75
Dairylea Cheese Spread, Kraft		28	1	80
	triangle			40
Devilled Ham Country Pot Paste, Shippams		35	1¼	70
Fish paste, average		28	1	47
Gold Dairy Spread, St Ivel		28	1	85
Golden syrup, average	1 tablespoon			60
Ham & Cheese Toast Topper, Heinz		28	1	55

	g	oz	Cal.
Ham Spread, Prince's	28	1	124
Ham & Beef Paste, Shippams	35	1¼	70
Honey, average	28	1	28
Honey Bear Spread, Bear Brand	28	1	82
Liver & Bacon Paste, Shippams	35	1¼	67
Malt extract, average	28	1	86
Marmite	28	1	2
Meat paste, average	28	1	61
Melbury Cheese Spread, Dairy Crest	28	1	89
Mushroom & Bacon Toast Topper tinned	130	4½	96
Peanut Butter: average	28	1	180
Boots	28	1	170
Gales Crunchy	28	1	170
Sun-Pat	28	1	177
Pear & Apple Spread, Harmony	28	1	73
Pilchard & Tomato Paste, Shippams	28	1	120
Sandwich Spread, Heinz	28	1	70
Sardine & Tomato Spread, Sainsbury	35	1¼	55
Smokey Bacon Spread, Prince's	53	1¾	120

		g	oz	Cal.
Tastex Spread, Granose		28	1	62
Whip Topping, Rich's	30ml/1 fl oz			20

VEGETABLES

		g	oz	Cal.
Ackee		28	1	43
Artichoke, boiled		28	1	3
Asparagus, boiled		28	1	3
Aubergine, uncooked		28	1	4
Avocado pear, weighed without stone		28	1	26
Baked beans:				
Chef, with hamburgers		28	1	34
Crosse & Blackwell, in tomato sauce		28	1	27
Heinz, in tomato sauce		28	1	20
Spar		28	1	24
with pork sausages, average		28	1	35
Bamboo shoots, average	tinned	28	1	5
Beans:				
aduki: boiled		28	1	94
raw weight		28	1	94
baked, average	tinned	28	1	20
black eye: boiled		28	1	38
raw		28	1	93

		g	oz	Cal.
broad: boiled		28	1	14
raw		28	1	10
buttered: boiled		28	1	77
raw		28	1	77
cannellini, average	tinned	28	1	25
French, boiled		28	1	10
flageolet, boiled		28	1	32
haricot: boiled		28	1	26
raw		28	1	77
lima, raw, dry weight		28	1	92
mung, raw, dry weight		28	1	92
red kidney: average	tinned	28	1	25
raw, dry weight		28	1	77
runner: boiled		28	1	5
raw		28	1	7
snap, raw, green		28	1	10
soya: boiled		28	1	50
raw, dry weight		28	1	108
Beetroot: boiled		28	1	12
raw		28	1	8
Tesco	tinned	28	1	39
Beetroot in Vinaigrette, St Michael		28	1	47
Broccoli: boiled		28	1	5
raw		28	1	1
Broccoli Spears, frozen, Findus		28	1	9
Broccoli Stir Fry, St Michael		28	1	8

	g	oz	Cal.
Brussels Sprouts: boiled	28	1	5
frozen, Ross	28	1	11
raw	28	1	7
Butter beans: Batchelor's	223	7¾	151
Tesco	28	1	27
Cabbage:			
boiled	28	1	4
raw	28	1	6
red, pickled, average	28	1	3
red, raw	28	1	6
Savoy, boiled	28	1	3
spring, boiled	28	1	2
Carrots: boiled	28	1	5
raw	28	1	6
Smedley's tinned	28	1	5
Cassava, fresh	28	1	43
Cauliflower:			
boiled	28	1	3
florets, frozen, Ross	28	1	7
raw	28	1	4
Cauliflower Stir-fry, frozen, St Michael	28	1	13
Celeriac: boiled	28	1	4
raw	28	1	8
Celery: boiled	28	1	1
braised	28	1	2
raw	28	1	2

		g	oz	Cal.
Chick peas: boiled		28	1	42
raw		28	1	91
Chicory, raw		28	1	3
Chinese leaves, boiled		28	1	2
Cucumber, raw		28	1	3
Endive		28	1	3
Garden Peas, Morton's	tin	300	10½	115
Garlic				0
Green Beans, Green Giant		283	10	50
Gherkins, pickled, Epicure		28	1	5
Haricots Verts, frozen, Findus		28	1	19
Horseradish, raw		28	1	17
Kidney Beans, Green Giant	tin	432	15¼	504
Leek, raw		28	1	9
Lentils: brown, boiled		28	1	32
brown, uncooked		28	1	104
Lettuce		28	1	3
Marrow: boiled		28	1	2
raw		28	1	5
Mexicorn, Green Giant	tinned	198	7	182
Mint, fresh		28	1	3
Mixed Chinese Vegetables	tinned	38	1¼	175

		g	oz	Cal.
Mixed Vegetables, frozen, Findus		28	1	16
Mushrooms: fried in butter		28	1	62
raw		28	1	2
Mushrooms in Brine, Chesswood		213	7½	15
Mushy Peas: Batchelor's	tinned	300	10½	145
Morton's		300	10½	228
Mustard & cress		28	1	3
Okra, raw		28	1	5
Onion:				
boiled		28	1	4
cocktail	each			1
fried		28	1	98
pickled: average	each			5
Epicure		28	1	4
Sweet, Epicure		28	1	7
raw		28	1	7
rings: in batter, fried, average		28	1	145
Ross		28	1	65
Safeway	packet	50	1¾	260
Sainsbury	packet	50	1¾	160
spring	each			3
Original Mixed Vegetables, Bird's Eye		28	1	15
Parsley, fresh		28	1	6

	g	oz	Cal.
Parsnip: boiled	28	1	15
roasted	28	1	30
Peas:			
dried: boiled	28	1	29
raw	28	1	81
fresh: boiled	28	1	14
raw	28	1	18
mange tout: boiled	28	1	12
raw	28	1	16
split: dried and boiled	28	1	33
dried, raw	28	1	87
tinned: garden	28	1	13
processed	28	1	23
processed, Batchelor's	149	5¼	96
processed, Smedley's	142	5	95
Peas & Baby Carrots, frozen, Bird's Eye	28	1	10
Peas & Carrots, Smedley's tinned	425	15	165
Pepper, green, purple, red or yellow	28	1	4
Petits Pois à la Française, St Michael	28	1	20
Petit Pois, Tesco tinned	100	3¾	52
Pimento, tinned in brine, average	28	1	6
Plantain: green, boiled	28	1	35
green, raw	28	1	32
ripe, fried in butter	28	1	75

		g	oz	Cal.
Potato:				
baked, whole		28	1	23
boiled, new		28	1	21
chips: Safeway, frozen		28	1	40
Tesco, frozen crinkle		28	1	56
Wimpy	portion			250
Croquettes: Findus, frozen		28	1	26
Sainsbury, frozen	each			20
Crunchies, Sainsbury		50	1¾	240
Grill, Findus		28	1	40
New, Gateway	tinned	28	1	18
Noisettes, Ross	each			52
Oven Crunches, Ross		28	1	48
Pommes Noisettes, Jus-Rol	each			10
Sauté, Findus		28	1	30
Scoops, Gateway		28	1	170
sweet: boiled		28	1	24
raw		28	1	26
Radish	each			2
Salsify, boiled		28	1	5
Saucy Spuds, Crosse & Blackwell		425	15	245
Sauerkraut	tinned	28	1	5
Saveloy, raw	each			230
Seakale, boiled		28	1	2
Spinach: boiled		28	1	9
leaf, Smedley's	tin	269	9½	55
raw		28	1	7
Spring greens		28	1	3

	g	oz	Cal.
Spring onions, raw	28	1	10
Stir Fry Vegetables with Sweet & Sour Sauce, St Michael	340	12	310
Surprise Beans, Batchelor's	33	1¾	90
Surprise Peas, Batchelor's	40	1½	110
Swedes: boiled	28	1	5
raw	28	1	6
Sweetcorn: cob, medium size			155
frozen, average	28	1	25
in brine tinned	28	1	22
Sweetcorn Niblets, Green Giant tin	98	7	170
Swiss Style Potatocakes, Findus each			80
Tomato: fried	28	1	19
raw	28	1	4
Turnips: boiled	28	1	4
raw	28	1	6
Watercress	28	1	4
Whole Asparagus Spears, Green Giant tinned	425	16	93
Yams, boiled	28	1	32

VEGETARIAN DISHES

	g	oz	Cal.
Cauliflower, Stir-fry, frozen, St Michael	28	1	13

		g	oz	Cal.
Chop Suey:				
Batchelors's Vesta Meal	portion			478
Beanfeast		28	1	77
Chow Mein, Bachelor's Vesta Meal	portion			315
Mexican Bean Stew, Granose	tinned	425	15	525
Nut Brawn, Granose	tinned	284	10	600
Pease Pudding, Sainsbury		439	15½	390
Soya:				
bean curd		28	1	15
bean in brine, Granose		425	15	725
bean with onion, Oxo	packet			385
mince with vegetable, Direct Foods, Protovec Menu		28	1	100
bean pâté, Granose		205	7¼	270
Vegebanger Mix, Realeat, made up	packet			293
Vegeburger Mix, Realeat, made up	packet			240
Vegelinks, Granose		425	15	710
Vegetable Curry:				
Mr Fritzi's Frys		28	1	103
Vesta	2 portions			200
Vegetable Goulash, Mr Fritzi's Frys		28	1	103

DRINK

	ml	fl oz	Cal.

BEER AND LAGER

	ml	fl oz	Cal.
Arctic Lite Lager, Allied Breweries	284	½pt	82
Carling Black Label, Bass Charrington	568	1pt	195
Carlsberg de Luxe, Carlsberg	275	9¾	122
Carlsberg Special Brew, Carlsberg	275	9¾	204
Carlsen Lite, Carlsberg	275	9¾	85
Colt 45, Courage	440	15½	185
Country Strong Bitter, Ruddles	568	1pt	245
Draught ale: bitter	568	1pt	180
mild	568	1pt	140
Draught Stout, Guinness	568	1pt	184
English Ale, Whitbread	284	½pt	105
Export Lager, Watney's	284	½pt	96
Export Ale, Whitbread	454	16	162
Extra Stout, Guinness	284	½pt	100
Forest Brown Ale, Whitbread	440	15½	84
Gerstel Low Alcohol Ale, Courage	330	11½	69
Heineken Lager, Whitbread	275	9¾	87

		ml	fl oz	Cal.
Heldenbrau Lager, Whitbread		275	9¾	70
Hemeling Lager, Bass Charrington		284	½pt	78
Hof Lager, Carlsberg		275	9¾	110
Hofmeister Lager, Courage		275	9¾	96
Ind Coope Double Diamond, Allied Breweries		284	½pt	115
Ind Coope Longlife		284	½pt	101
John Courage	bottle	275	9¾	110
Kronenbourg Lager: Courage		275	9¾	110
Guinness		284	½pt	110
Lamont Pilson Strong Lager, Bass Charrington		284	½pt	111
Limeade & Lager, Corona	can	330	11½	102
Lite Ale, Whitbread		440	15½	76
London Pride, Fullers Beers		284	½pt	105
Mackeson Stout, Whitbread		440	15½	114
McEwan's Export, Scottish & Newcastle		440	15½	150
McEwan's Pale Ale, Scottish & Newcastle		440	15½	103
McEwan's Lager, Scottish & Newcastle		440	15½	132

		ml	fl oz	Cal.
Newcastle Amber Ale, Scottish & Newcastle		275	9¾	70
Newcastle Brown Ale, Scottish & Newcastle		440	15½	170
Pilsner, Carlsberg Lager		275	9¾	76
Red & Special Beer, Watney's	can	440	15½	70
Satsenbrau, Guinness Lager		284	½pt	106
Shandy: Barr		250	8¾	64
Britvic Slimsta Range		275	9¾	14
Corona	tinned	140	¼pt	35
'68 Carlsberg Lager		330	11½	200
Skol Lager, Allied Breweries	draught	284	½pt	92
	tinned	275	9¾	75
Stella Artois, Whitbread Lager	tinned	330	11½	138
Stones Bitter, Bass Charrington	canned	545	16	172
Tankard, Whitbread		284	½pt	100
Tartan Bitter, Scottish & Newcastle	tinned	440	15½	138
Tartan Special, Scottish & Newcastle	tinned	440	15½	138
Tennent's, Bass Lager	draught	284	½pt	92
Tennent's Extra, Bass Lager	tinned	440	16	175

		ml	fl oz	Cal.
Toby Brown Ale, Bass Charrington	bottle	275	9¾	70
Toby Light Ale, Bass Charrington	bottle	275	9¾	70
Worthington E Beer, Bass Charrington		284	½pt	100
Worthington White Shield Beer, Bass Charrington		275	9¾	130
Younger's Lite Ale, Scottish & Newcastle	tinned	440	15½	106
Younger's Sweet Stout, Scottish & Newcastle	bottle	275	9¾	65

CIDER

Autumn Gold Cider, Taunton	bottled	275	9¾	100
Dry Blackthorn Cider, Taunton		275	9¾	95
Exhibition Dry Cider, Taunton		284	½pt	150
Exhibition Sweet Cider, Taunton		284	½pt	182
Farmhouse Cider, Coates		284	½pt	151
Festival Vat Cider, Coates		284	½pt	135
Lite Cider, Gayner's		284	½pt	79
Olde English Cider, Gayner's		284	½pt	124

		ml	fl oz	Cal.
Pomagne:				
Bulmer's Dry Cider		284	½pt	150
Bulmer's Sweet Cider		284	½pt	184
Pommetta:				
Gayner's Dry Cider		284	½pt	152
Gayner's Sweet Cider		284	½pt	194
Pommia:				
Taunton Dry Cider		284	½pt	156
Taunton Sweet Cider		284	½pt	192
Scrumpy, Coates Cider		284	½pt	126
Somerset, Coates Cider		284	½pt	90
Special Vat, Taunton Cider		275	9¾	112
Strongbow, Bulmer's Cider		284	½pt	101
Woodpecker Cider, Bulmer's		284	½pt	100

CRUSHES

		ml	fl oz	Cal.
Apple Crush, Sainsbury		330	11½	130
Bitter Lemon Crush:				
Britvic	bottle	113	4	50
Britvic Slimsta Range	bottle	180	6	0
Blackcurrant Crush, Britvic				
Slimsta Range	bottle	180	6	5
Cariba, Schweppes		330	11½	115

		ml	fl oz	Cal.
Grapefruit Crush, Britvic Slimsta Range	bottle	180	6	11
Lime & Lemon Crush, Britvic	bottle	180	6	85
Orange Crush:				
Britvic	bottle	180	6	84
Britvic Slimsta Range	bottle	180	6	12
Pineapple Crush, Britvic Slimsta Range	bottle	180	6	8
Sparkling Orange Crush, Schweppes		250	8¾	115
Strawberry Crush, Sainsbury		330	11½	130

HOT DRINKS

		Cal.
Bournvita, Cadbury	1 teaspoon	22
Bovril:	1 teaspoon	12
	cube	10
Maxpax Vending Machine	each	15
Build Up, Carnation	sachet	130
Chocolate Drink, Maxpax	each	66
Chocolate Flavoured Drink, Drinkmaster	each	70
Chocolate Flavoured Ovaltine	1 teaspoon	16

		ml	fl oz	Cal.
Cocoa without sugar	I teaspoon			20
Cocoa powder, average		28	I	15
Coffee & Chicory Essence, Camp	I teaspoon			10
Coffee beans, average, ground & infused		28g	I oz	0
Coffee: instant, average powder or granules, without water		28	I	28
Maxpax: black with sugar	each			24
with milk, no sugar	each			15
Dandelion Coffee, Lane's Health Products		100g	3½oz	320
Double Top, Nestlé		28	I	50
Drinking chocolate: average	I teaspoon			28
Cadbury	I teaspoon			22
Nisa	I teaspoon			20
Elevenses, Nestlé	I heaped teaspoon			5
Horlicks Chocolate Malted Drink, Beecham	sachet	32g	1½oz	113
Horlicks Malted Drink, Beecham	sachet	32g	1½oz	122
Hot Chocolate, Wimpy	each			230

		ml	fl oz	Cal.
Hot Chocolate Mix, Carnation		29g	1oz	110
Lemon Tea:				
Drinkmaster Vending Machine	each			40
Maxpax	each			35
Low Fat Drinking Chocolate Granules, St Michael		28g	1oz	102
Malted Chocolate Flavour Drink, Batchelor's Cup-a-Time	sachet			125
Malted Drink, Boots	1 teaspoon			21
Malted Milk, Safeway	1 teaspoon			35
Malt Flavour Drink, Batchelor's Cup-a-Time	sachet			132
Marvel, Cadbury, dry	1 teaspoon			6
Milk:				
fresh, pasteurised, Silver Top		568	1pt	380
instant, Tesco: dry		28g	1oz	25
made up		575	1pt	192
Milo, Nestlé	1 teaspoon			24
Milquick, St Ivel	1 teaspoon			6
Nesquik, Nestlé	mug			180
Ovaltine, Wander: granules	1 teaspoon			20
powder	sachet	20g	¾oz	80
Oxo Beef Drink, Brooke Bond Oxo	1 teaspoon			4

	ml	fl oz	Cal.
Oxo Chicken Cube, Brooke Bond Oxo	cube		14
Slim Choc, Carnation	sachet		41
Tea, Drinkmaster Vending Machine: white with sugar	each		40
white, no sugar	each		10
Tea-Mate, Carnation	1 teaspoon		10
White Freeze-dried Coffee, Maxpax	each		21
White Tea, no sugar, Maxpax	each		9

JUICES

		ml	fl oz	Cal.
Apple Juice:				
Copella	carton	200	7	86
Del Monte	carton	142	¼pt	84
Gateway		100	3½	38
Southern Gold Long Life		140	¼pt	64
Apple & Honey Drink, Hi-Fruit Still Fruit Drinks		28	1	14
Barley Cup, Ridpath Pek	1 teaspoon			6
Beetroot Juice, Biotta	1 litre			400
Carrot Juice, Biotta		100	4	35
Coconut Milk, fresh		28	1	6

		ml	fl oz	Cal.
Five Alive Citrus Juice, Coca Cola		200	7	95
Five Alive Tropical, Coca Cola		200	7	85
Florida Grapefruit Juice, Birds Eye reconstituted		140	¼pt	36
Florida Orange Juice, Birds Eye reconstituted		140	¼pt	43
Good Start Juice, Libby's		140	¼pt	51
Grapefruit Juice:				
Britvic	bottle	113	4	62
Britvic '55'	bottle	180	6	90
Club	bottle	113	4	65
Express Dairies		140	¼pt	43
Just Juice		140	¼pt	50
Southern Gold, Longlife		140	¼pt	55
Grape Juice: Bulmer's		140	¼pt	66
Schloers		250	8¾	125
Hi-C Orange Juice, Coca Cola		200	7	91
Jaffa Orange Juice, St Michael		200	7	60
Natural Apple Juice, Martlett		100	4	40
Orange Juice:				
average, unsweetened		28	1	11
Britvic		113	4	50
Club, sweetened	bottle	113	4	61
Club, unsweetened	bottle	113	4	57
Express Dairies		100	4	35

		ml	fl oz	Cal.
Heinz		120	4¼	56
Libby's unsweetened		140	¼pt	45
Robinson's, Ready Drink		250	8¾	92
Waitrose		200	7	70
Zing		180	6¼	89
Orange, Apple & Passion Fruit, Del Monte		140	¼pt	43
Pineapple Juice:				
Britvic '55'	tinned	250	8¾	136
Canada Dry, Sodastream	bottled	113	4	55
Club	bottled	113	4	62
Heinz	bottled	120	4¼	71
Sainsbury		140	¼pt	62
Prune juice, average		28	1	26
Red Grape Juice, Schloer	carton	250	8¾	125
Sun & Rise Juice, Kellogg's:				
lemon, reconstituted		113	4	45
orange, pineapple, blackcurrant, reconstituted		113	4	50
Sunfruit Juice, St Michael		140	¼pt	68
Tomato Juice: average		28	1	6
Club	bottle	113	4	25
Unsweetened Orange, Club	bottle	113	4	48

	ml	fl oz	Cal.

MILK SHAKES

		ml	fl oz	Cal.
Banana Milk Shake, Crusha		28	1	38
Chocolate Shake, McDonald's	each			380
Strawberry Milk, St Michael		150	6½	140
Strawberry Shake, McDonald's	each			350
Thick Shake, Wimpy	each			250
Two Shakes Chocolate Drink Mix, Kellogg's	sachet			75
Vanilla Shake, McDonald's	each			350
Whippsy, Wimpy	each			222

NON-ALCOHOLIC DRINKS

			ml	fl oz	Cal.
Apple & Blackcurrant Drink, Robinson			250	8¾	112
Appletise, Schweppes		bottled	180	7	75
Beer Shandy, non-alcoholic, Minster		can	270	9½	70
Bitter Lemon:	Canada Dry	bottle	175	6	70
	Club	bottle	113	4	30
		bottle	180	7	50

		ml	fl oz	Cal.
Hunts, sparkling		140	¼pt	50
Sainsbury		140	¼pt	45
Spar		100	4	43
Waitrose		100	4	35
Cherryade, Whites		28	1	6
Cherry Coca Cola	can	330	11½	140
Coca Cola, Coca Cola		330	11½	130
Coke: Pizza Express	each			110
Wimpy	large			133
Cola: Boots low calorie drink		330	11½	5
Britvic		110	4	43
Britvic Slimsta Range		180	6	8
Sainsbury		280	½pt	120
Cream Soda, Whites		28	1	5
Danish Life, non-alcoholic lager		320	1	57
Diet Coca Cola, Coca Cola		330	11½	0
Diet Pepsi, Pepsi Cola		330	11½	0
Dry Ginger Ale: average		100	4	14
Safeway		140	¼pt	5
Waitrose		140	¼pt	28
Duo Club		180	6	72
Fanta Cream Soda, Coca Cola	1 litre		1¾pt	292
Fanta Ginger Beer, Coca Cola	1 litre		1¾pt	310
Fanta Lemonade, Coca Cola	tin	330	11½	87

		ml	fl oz	Cal.
Fanta Limeade, Coca Cola	1 litre		1¾pt	240
Fanta Orange Crush, Coca Cola		330	11½	112
Fanta Raspberryade, Coca Cola	1 litre		1¾pt	296
Ginger Beer: average		28	1	11
Britvic	bottle	180	6	72
Corona	bottle	140	¼pt	40
Schweppes	bottle	170	5½	60
Hi-Fruit Apple & Honey Drink, Schweppes		250	8½	126
Hi-Fruit Caribbean Drink, Schweppes		250	8½	120
Hi-Fruit Orange Drink, Schweppes		250	8½	116
Indian Tonic Water: Hunts		140	¼pt	34
Idris		140	¼pt	34
Irn Bru, Barr		250	8¾	100
Irn Bru, low calorie, Barr		330	11½	16
Jusoda Orange Drink, Barr	bottle	250	8¾	89
Lemonade:				
Barr		250	8¾	76
Boots Shapers	can	330	11½	0
Britvic	bottle	113	4	34
Britvic Slimsta Range	bottle	170	6	5
Canada Dry Slim Drink		175	6¼	0
Whites		100	3½	20

		ml	fl oz	Cal.
Lemonade Shandy, Schweppes		275	½pt	68
Lemon Drink, Drinkmaster Vending Machine	each			58
Lemon Countrytime Drink, Maxpax	each			25
Lemon & Limeade, Sodastream, made up		230	8	63
Lemonade Shandy, Safeway	can	330	11½	128
Limeade, Tesco		140	¼pt	32
Lilt, Coca Cola		330	11½	162
Lucozade	bottle	250	8½	177
Mineral water, average				0
Orange & Apple Drink, Robinson's		250	8¾	90
Orange & Apricot Drink, Waitrose		140	¼pt	58
Orange Drink:				
Boots low calorie drink	can	330	11½	6
Drinkmaster Vending Machine	each			50
Orange Sixty, Rawlings		180	6	102
Pineapple Sixty, Rawlings	bottled	180	6	102
Pepsi Cola, Pepsi Cola	tinned	330	11½	145
Raspberry, Zing		180	6¼	80

		ml	fl oz	Cal.
Russchian, Schweppes	bottle	500	17½	115
Seven up:		341	12	130
diet		341	12	0
Shandy: Barr		250	8¾	64
Britvic Slimsta Range		275	9¾	14
Corona	tinned	140	¼pt	35
Slimgard Liquid Meal				
Replacement, strawberry	meal			325
Slimline:				
American Ginger Ale,				
Schweppes	bottle	180	6¼	0
Bitter Lemon, Schweppes	bottled	180	6¼	4
Lemonade & Beer Shandy,				
Schweppes	bottle	330	11½	19
Lemonade, Schweppes	bottle	180	6¼	0
Sparkling Orange Crush,				
Schweppes	bottle	330	11½	6
Tonic Water, Schweppes	bottle	180	6¼	0
Sparkling Bitter Lemon Drink:				
Hunts	bottle	140	¼pt	47
Hunts low calorie	bottle	250	8¾	0
Sparkling Blackcurrantade,				
Corona	bottle	140	¼pt	36
Sparkling Cherryade, Corona	bottle	250	8¾	63
Sparkling Cola Drink, Corona	bottle	250	8¾	103
Sparkling Cream Soda, Corona	bottle	140	¼pt	35

		ml	fl oz	Cal.
Sparkling Grapefruit Drink, Tango	tinned	330	11½	140
Sparkling Iron Brew, Corona		140	¼pt	28
Sparkling Lemon & Lime Drink, Hunts low calorie	tinned	250	8¾	9
Sparkling Limeade, Corona	tinned	140	¼pt	35
Sparkling Orangeade, Corona	tinned	140	¼pt	41
Sparkling Orange Drink, Hunts low calorie	tinned	250	8¾	10
Sparkling Orange & Pineapple Drink, Tango	tinned	330	11½	146
Strawberry Drink, Cresta		250	8¾	90
Strike Cola, Barr	bottled	250	8¾	85
Tab, Coca Cola	tinned			0
Tizer, Barr	tin	250	8¾	100
	tin	330	11½	130
Tomato Cocktail, Club	bottle	113	4	25
Tonic Water:				
Canada Dry	bottle	175	6¼	40
Canada Dry Slim Drink	bottle	175	6¼	0
Schweppes Slimline Drink	bottle	180	6¼	0
Vimto, Barr	tinned	250	8¾	66
Wine, de-alcoholised	average glass	115	4	35

		ml	fl oz	Cal.

SLIMMERS' AND HEALTH DRINKS

		ml	fl oz	Cal.
Bitter Lemon:				
Boots low calorie	can	330	11½	5
Hunts low calorie		140	¼pt	5
Bittersweet sparkling low-calorie drinks	can	250	8¾	10
Schweppes Slimline	bottle	180	6¼	5
Sainsbury low calorie		140	¼pt	0
Butterscotch, Complan	serving	57g	2oz	250
Chocolate Complan, Complan		57g	2oz	252
Chocolate Flavour Cup-a-Time, Batchelor's	sachet			120
Cola: Boots low calorie		330	11½	5
Britvic Slimsta Range		180	6	8
Dandelion & Burdock, Whites		28	1	7
Diet Coca Cola, Coca Cola		330	11½	0
Diet Lemonade, Whites		250	8¾	5
Diet Pepsi Cola, Pepsi Cola		330	11½	0
Diet Ginger Ale, Safeway		140	¼pt	5
Grapefruit C, Libby's		140	¼pt	54
Irn Bru, low calorie, Barr		330	11½	16

		ml	fl oz	Cal.
Kaltenberg Diet Pils, Whitbread		284	½pt	119
Lemonade:				
Boots Shapers	can	330	11½	3
Britvic Slimsta Range	bottle	180	6	4
Canada Dry Slim Drink		175	6	0
Lemon & Lime, Boots low calorie drink	can	330	11½	5
Lemon Squash, Roses, diabetic		28	1	0
Low Calorie:				
American Ginger Ale, Hunts		140	¼pt	0
Bitter Lemon, Hunts		140	¼pt	0
Bitter Orange, Hunts		142	¼pt	4
Indian Tonic Water		140	¼pt	0
Jaffa Lemon Drink, Tesco		28	1	5
Orange Crush, St Michael		250	8¾	9
Tonic, Club		113	4	0
Tonic Water, Sainsbury		140	¼pt	0
Orange Drink, Boots low calorie drink	can	330	11½	6
Pils, Holstein Diabetic Lager		270	9	106
Plamil C Soya Milk Concentrate		30	1	29
Pranavite Slim, HTB (UK) Milk Protein drink	sachet			200
Seven Up, diet		341	12	0
Shandy, Britvic Slimsta Range		275	9	14

		ml	fl oz	Cal.
Slim Choc, Carnation	sachet			41
Slimline:				
American Ginger Ale,				
Schweppes	bottled	180	6¼	0
Bitter Lemon, Schweppes	bottled	180	6¼	4
Lemonade & Beer Shandy,				
Schweppes	bottle	330	11½	19
Lemonade, Schweppes	bottle	180	6¼	0
Sparkling Orange Crush,				
Shweppes	bottled	330	11¼	6
Tonic Water, Schweppes	bottle	180	6¼	0
Soya Milk, Granose		140	¼pt	74
Sparkling Bitter Lemon Drink,				
Hunts low calorie	bottle	250	8¾	0
Sparkling Dandelion & Burdock,				
Corona	bottled	140	¼pt	31
Sparkling Lemon & Lime Drink,				
Hunts low calorie	tinned	250	8¾	9
Sparkling Orange Drink, Hunts				
low calorie	tinned	250	8¾	10
Strawberry Milk Drink, low fat,				
Unigate		568	1pt	335
Tonic Water:				
Canada Dry Slim Drink	bottle	175	6¼	0
Schweppes Slimline Drink	bottle	180	6¼	0

SPIRITS, LIQUEURS AND FORTIFIED WINES

	ml	fl oz	Cal.
Advocaat	25	⅙ gill	65
Apricot Brandy	25	⅙ gill	60
Brandy	25	⅙ gill	50
Calvados	25	⅙ gill	65
Campari	25	⅙ gill	57
Champagne: average	110	4	80
Safeway	110	4	105
Chartreuse	25	⅙ gill	100
Cherry brandy	25	⅙ gill	64
Cinzano: Bianco	50	⅓ gill	82
Rosso	50	⅓ gill	76
Cointreau	25	⅙ gill	85
Cream sherry	50	⅓ gill	65
Crème de cassis	25	⅙ gill	60
Crème de menthe	25	⅙ gill	82
Crocodillo	bottle		61
Curaçao	25	⅙ gill	70
Drambuie	25	⅙ gill	80
Dry sherry	50	⅓ gill	59

		ml	fl oz	Cal.
Dubonnet: dry		50	⅓ gill	55
red		50	⅓ gill	70
Frattelli Bianco, Vermouth		50	⅓ gill	74
Galliano		25	⅙ gill	76
Gin		25	⅙ gill	55
Ginger wine		113	4	185
Goldwell's Calypso, low alcohol drink	bottle			102
Goldwell's Wee McGlen, low alcohol drink	bottle			102
Grand Marnier		25	⅙ gill	80
Kirsch		25	⅙ gill	47
Kümmel		25	⅙ gill	75
Malibu		25	⅙ gill	51
Margarita, Shakers	bottle	160	6½	160
Martini Bianco		50	⅓ gill	67
Martini Extra Dry		50	⅓ gill	67
Martini Rosé		50	⅓ gill	85
Martini Rosso		50	⅓ gill	91
Pernod		25	⅙ gill	61
Pimms No 1 Cup		50	⅓ gill	98
Pina Colada, St Michael		250	8¾	230

	ml	fl oz	Cal.
Port	25	⅙ gill	36
Rum	25	⅙ gill	55
Sherry: cream	50	⅓ gill	63
dry	50	⅓ gill	54
medium	50	⅓ gill	58
Strega	25	⅙ gill	77
Tequila	25	⅙ gill	50
Tia Maria	25	⅙ gill	75
Vodka	25	⅙ gill	53
Whisky	25	⅙ gill	50

SQUASHES

		ml	fl oz	Cal.
Barley Water, Robinson's, undiluted		28	1	30
Beetroot squash		100	3½	40
Blackcurrant: Cresta		28	1	10
	1 litre		1¾pt	50
	bottle	250	8¾	90
Drinkmaster Vending Machine	each			30
Maxpax	each			25

	ml	fl oz	Cal.
Blackcurrant Drink:			
Waitrose	200	7	90
C Vit, undiluted	28	1	60
Ribena, undiluted	28	1	83
Caribbean Fruit Drink, Hi-Fruit			
Still Fruit Drink	28	1	14
Lemon Barley Water,			
St Clements	28	1	30
Lemon Squash, undiluted:			
average	28	1	30
Roses Diabetic	28	1	0
Ribena:			
Baby, all flavours	28	1	90
	100	3½	316
concentrated	28	1	65
ready to drink,			
Beecham	250	8¾	150
Whole grapefruit drink,			
diluted with water, average	28	1	30
Whole lemon drink, diluted			
with water, average	28	1	26
Whole orange drink, diluted			
with water, average	28	1	32

	ml	fl oz	Cal.

SYRUPS AND CORDIALS

	ml	fl oz	Cal.
Banana Syrup, Rayner/Burgess	28	1	61
Blackcurrant Cordial, Corona, undiluted	100	3½	100
Blackcurrant Flavour Cordial, Corona, undiluted	28	1	60
Chocolate Milk Shake Syrup, Crusha	28	1	47
Ginger cordial, undiluted	28	1	27
Grenadine syrup	28	1	72
Pineapple milk shake syrup	1 tablespoon		20
Raspberry Milk Shake Syrup, Crusha	28	1	30
Rosehip syrup, undiluted	100	3½	232
	1 tablespoon		95
Rose Grape Juice, Shloer	225	7½	125
Strawberry cordial, undiluted	28	1	34
Strawberry Milk Shake Syrup, Crusha	28	1	30

		ml	fl oz	Cal.

WINES

		ml	fl oz	Cal.
Champagne	average glass	115	4	80
De-alcoholised	average glass	115	4	35
Dry red	average glass	115	4	80
Dry white	average glass	115	4	75
Rosé	average glass	115	4	85
Sparkling	average glass	115	4	90
Sweet red	average glass	115	4	100
Sweet white	average glass	115	4	105